The Last Philosophy

Don Cupitt

The Last Philosophy

SCM PRESS LTD

0 334 02586 9

First published 1995
by SCM Press Ltd
26–30 Tottenham Road, London N1 4BZ

Typeset at The Spartan Press Ltd,
Lymington, Hants
and printed in Great Britain by
Biddles Ltd, Guildford and King's Lynn

For Sally

Contents

Preface

This book stands a little apart from what I have written hitherto. It marks a – perhaps only temporary – change of tack.

For many years I have been writing philosophical theology from a standpoint within the Christian tradition, asking how we today are to interpret, modify and appropriate what has come down to us from the past. Not an easy task, because the crisis of faith in the modern world is so severe, and in order to tackle it I had to develop a number of philosophical ideas. These grew and changed from book to book. 'The truth is in the movement', I used to say cheerfully, meaning that as I went on, surely, what I was doing and why would gradually become clear.

It didn't. Indeed, it began to seem that my philosophy, instead of making my theology easier to understand and accept, was having exactly the opposite effect. Perhaps I ought to pause now, and to articulate and systematize my philosophy?

Easier said than done, for as a subject philosophy is itself *also* in crisis, and when I try to set them all out in systematic but non-technical terms, I think ruefully that my philosophical ideas turn out to be, if anything, even more objectionably heretical than my theological ones.

My difficulty is a little like Wittgenstein's. I want to centre religious and philosophical thinking in the here and now, in the world of ordinary language and ordinary life. But to do that I find I've got to change a number of our most deeply-rooted ideas – ideas about thought and reality, about the self and the way it is related to its world, and so on. So it looks as if, like Wittgenstein, I'm claiming that I don't want to change anything – but finding that in order to make good that claim I've got to change a great deal.

It seems a paradox; but my answer will have to be that we are in difficulties, both in religion and philosophy, because we are

I

clinging so obstinately to concepts and ways of thinking left over from the past, and now hopelessly unsuitable. No doubt the new 'expressionist' world-view that I am here proposing will seem very queer at first, but I can only invite the reader to try it on like a suit of clothes in a shop. Try it for fit. Turn around. See how it feels.

This book, then, aims to be a democratic philosophy of human life. *Democratic*, in the sense that whereas the main tradition of 'great' philosophy from Plato to Nietzsche was written by and for a very small élite only, we now need to democratize philosophy. We need to leave behind us the idea that some small group of priests, or of philosophers, or of scientists, has the right and the duty to tell the rest of us what to think and how we should live.

When we go democratic, we join not only Wittgenstein, but also a few others like perhaps William James and Feuerbach, in trying to set philosophy's centre of gravity firmly in the midst of ordinary life. Hence the phrase, philosophy of human life, and we make the point that although we may usefully consult the scientist, the philosopher and the priest, those professionals themselves were human beings before they became professionals. They too need to remember that their specialized technical vocabulary still has to be earthed, back into ordinary language and ordinary life. None of us can afford to forget that all the fancy metaphors of science, of philosophy and of religion have to refer back in the end to ordinariness and draw their meaning from it.

I say human *life*, rather than human being or human existence, because I want throughout to stress the strictly biological constraints upon our world-view. This is crucial for my version of non-realism, the main argument being that we are always inside our own biological life, that our vision of things is always subject to the constraints that our biology imposes, and that we have no access whatever to any other vision of things. The sort of fully independent validation of our view of things that realism would require is not available to us, and the only sort of world-view we'll ever have is a talking animal's world-view. But why complain? If we cannot find any fully-independent accreditation for our world-view, by the same token neither is it going to be *dis*credited; and with no basis either for cosmic self-congratulation or for cosmic grousing we are left saying simply that things are what they are. There's nothing wrong with being a talking animal. Here I'm trying, as so often before, to combine biological naturalism with linguistic naturalism. The idea is to reach a self-consistent, fully-critical and demythologized view of our life.

In the past, Western intellectuals usually considered that ordinary people should not be told the truth. Voltaire, for example, would send the servants out of the room when serious questions of religion and philosophy came up at the dinner table, an attitude that survives in the general assumption today that popular entertainment and popular writing have just got to be tabloid trash. Truth is not for the people: in Britain at least, what is 'popular' and what is 'quality' are two entirely separate markets.

I cannot accept that view or that policy. The education system does now try to democratize Darwinism and similar scientific theories, and it is obvious that many of 'the people' have already abandoned supernatural belief. I'd like to try to write a kind of philosophy that is genuinely accessible to the ordinary reader, while also being avant-garde, and holding nothing back.

Indeed, there is nothing to hold back, for biological naturalism and ordinary-language philosophy join in regarding the present scheme of things as final. The 'veil of sense' is not a veil at all, because there is nothing behind it. We would do well to forget the idea that this world is merely the ante-chamber to a greater world yet to come. On the contrary, this is our last life and these are our last bodies. Since there is no further Beyond, we are in effect *already* at the end of all things. From which it follows that any theology we may be able to reach here will be a kingdom-theology, and any religious lifestyle that we are likely to be able to end by recommending will be an 'eschatological' lifestyle, like the one Jesus teaches in the Sermon on the Mount. Live as if these are the last days; live as if at the end of the world; live as if you know for sure that sometime very soon everything's going to vanish forever and you along with it. Live like a child, or a seventy-year-old for whom life has become featherlight, pure grace, one day at a time, and who therefore feels completely free and happy. Live on the brink.

That's all right. Well, isn't it?

This essay may be read as completing the 'expressionist' series of books that began with *Creation out of Nothing* in 1990. I have been trying to start afresh. How can we reconstruct our world-picture after the very severe impact of post-structuralism and post-modernism, and after the searching criticism of our whole philosophical tradition that has come from Heidegger, Derrida and others? There seems no chance now of reinstating the older type of dogmatic metaphysics, oriented as it was towards ideas of substance, self-sameness and objective knowledge of eternal verities. So instead I have been thinking of Heraclitus, Nietzsche and Bataille, and of philosophies of process, action, conflict and expression. I have also been thinking of our life, and of the whole world's life, on the Big-Bang model of an outpouring discharge and scattering of dancing energies-read-as-signs. Everything is transient: passing, it is also passing away, and burning, it burns itself out.

Since the rise of the modern state and of modern science we have been influenced by a bureaucratic vision of the world and of our life: we look for a stable system maintained by the rule of law, and seek efficiency and conservation. But there was an older vision of things which emphasized gift, display, sacrifice and a good show, and I hope that something of it returns in these pages.

I am grateful to a number of students, including David Newns, Amelia Trotter, Phyllis Smart and Christopher Rowland (the Younger, that is) for their contributions and comments when they heard some of this book delivered as lectures. Members of the 'D' Society at Cambridge made useful comments when we debated the main argument. Hugh Rayment-Pickard and Petra Green read drafts of the text, and Linda Allen once again did the word-processing. Some technical terms do appear in the text, and are explained in a Glossary. I have also expanded the usual Index of Names into a 'prosopography'. (There really is such a word: it means a list of characters, with thumbnail sketches.) Once again, too, there is a certain amount of word-play in the text, and a few deliberate giveaways for you to spot.

D. C.
Cambridge, 1994

1. Philosophy and happiness

What draws people to philosophy, and why does the subject exist at all? Philosophers have offered various excuses for their strange preoccupation, but most claim that, in one way or another, philosophy does you good. According to Boethius and some others in antiquity, philosophy strengthens the soul and gives comfort in adversity. For the Schoolmen, philosophy was a good thing because it was the handmaid of theology; but David Hume valued it for the opposite reason. On his account philosophy is valuable not because it leads to theology but because it can rescue us from theology, which he sees as a violent and unhappy subject. There is much less conflict in the almost unpeopled regions where philosophers dwell.

Although many of the philosophers have spoken of the tranquil happiness their subject brings, they differ about how and why this happiness is achieved. Spinoza's joy is the rational satisfaction of someone who possesses absolute knowledge of universal rational necessity, a necessity that runs also through his own mind; whereas Bertrand Russell claims that philosophy is liberating in its very *un*certainty. He finds contentment in a free and undogmatic spirit of magnanimous cosmic wonder. Nietzsche is quite different again, for he sees the world as a theatre of violent, non-rational and conflicting forces, yet somehow finds his own way of turning life's cruelty into eternal joy. Queer: Spinoza's universe is thoroughly rational and Nietzsche's universe is utterly irrational – but both are philosophers of joy.

Other philosophers see their subject as tending at first to produce either scepticism or excessive and illusory belief. Good philosophy then gets the job of being a much-needed therapy for the disorders caused by bad philosophy. Thus Berkeley, Kant, Wittgenstein and others have seen philosophy as freeing our

5

thinking from disabling blockages and illusions. It is a style of argument that works to lead us back to sanity and ordinary life by persuading us that there is nothing wrong with everyday rationality and the limits of thought. Nothing is being held back from us; we are not missing anything. In this connection, consider the case of Hegel: in his highest speculative flights he experienced a sustained exaltation, whether godlike or manic, but in retrospect he himself feared that he might perhaps have run uncomfortably close to madness. And what indeed is the difference? For when we look again at some of the great systems of the past we are indeed puzzled to know what is the difference between cosmic joy and mania, between the highest metaphysical idealism and delirium, and between existential anxiety and neurotic anxiety.

Here we shall be proposing another view of the happiness to be found through philosophy. By philosophy I mean *Lebensphilosophie*, the philosophy of everyday life. Metaphysics in the future needs to be concerned with the *Lebenswelt*, the world of everyday life, for two main reasons. One is that after Darwin, and after the turn to language, we see that the world of everyday life conjured up by our language is the only real world there can be for us. There never was, and there never will be or can be, anything else. The other reason is that in our age of mass-production and mass-communications it can seem that everything around us is a mere copy or 'token', and nothing is an original. As happens in Andy Warhol's art, the infinite multiplication of images may have the effect of undermining people's sense of reality. In late capitalism we have lost the Logos (Greek: cosmic Reason); instead we have only packaging and logos (brand-images: say it aloud – loggoes). So, in the age when our thinking most needs to become completely reconciled to ordinariness, great economic and cultural forces are producing widespread feelings of unreality and worthlessness – and, in consequence, severe stress.

A corollary of all this is that in our age, which calls for a rational *Lebensphilosophie* powerful enough to persuade ordinary people of the sacred reality and moral worth of ordinary life, philosophy needs to become democratic. It can no longer afford the extreme élitism of its past. The subject will not survive and will not deserve to survive unless it can persuade the general taxpaying public that they need it, and that it can do them good – a lot of good.

A democratic philosophy of ordinary life then, which is concerned with happiness; and by happiness I mean *eudaimonia*, religious blessedness, a kind of happiness that does not desert us but remains with us even in the most extreme conditions we can experience. It may even be called 'eternal' happiness, or salvation.

This leads to the question of the relation between philosophy and religion. In antiquity it was close: every philosophy claimed to be a way to happiness, and Christianity itself was first preached to the gentile world, not as yet another religion, but as 'the one true philosophy'. In Asia philosophy and religion have remained close to each other, but in the West they have drifted apart. The long-term result is that both concerns have suffered severely: Western religion has become non-rational, and Western philosophy has almost no lay public. For the sake of their own survival, both subjects need to consider the possibility of a reconciliation. They have been too widely separated for too long, and it's killing them both. At present the public takes very little notice of either of them.

So the philosophy here presented will be a way to eternal happiness – that is, a happiness that can be relied upon not wholly to desert us, however bad things get – within the world of ordinary life. More than that, a happiness not just *within* the everyday world, but *with* the everyday world.

I don't claim that this is a region where philosophy is uniquely privileged. On the contrary, many people will tell of very simple mundane sources of happiness that, as they say, help to keep them sane. A classic image of this is the prisoner who takes daily comfort from his caged bird and his glimpse of a patch of blue sky. Yes, that's true: visual experience and contact with another living being can be sources of delight.

But philosophy has the advantage of being 'propositional' or 'textual'. By that I mean that it can be written and read, it can be made public: it can be argued, shared and even – as I hope – democratized. And if so, then it may again come to be seen as offering a generally-accessible way to salvation.

7

When re-conceived as a way to happiness within ordinariness and *with* ordinariness, philosophy does not offer any special supernatural or esoteric information. I haven't got any higher world or any deep structure of things to tell you about. In fact, you already know all that you need to know. All I am proposing to add is an artwork, a rationally-argued fiction that will give the reader a guiding picture. This picture, perhaps surprisingly, is intended to be comforting by being strictly reductionist and naturalistic. It will be an instructive diagram of the way things are with us. It teaches us to look upon ourselves, not as separate and therefore threatened beings, but as wholly interwoven with the whole process of things in such a way that we find we have no remaining cause for anxiety. We will find ourselves content to be a part of the flux from which we came and into which we return, which has produced us and which we also produce.

This realization – you may consider it Wittgensteinian, or perhaps Buddhist, if you insist – is comforting because it helps us to escape from various inherited disorders. The ways in which we have been taught to contrast mind and body, the self and the not-self, the sacred and the profane, the sign and the thing signified, the sensual and the spiritual, and appearance and reality, are here diagnosed as typical causes of our unhappiness. Such contrasts have fissured experience, have devalued tracts of life, and have tended to shut each person up in a private hell. We seek to undermine the contrasts, producing instead a monistic picture of the world as a one-level continuous process of ramifying, scattering energies, values and meanings. Rightly understood and used, this alternative picture will I hope be highly comforting, either because it exorcizes painful rival pictures, or because (as I hope some readers will find) it is productive of the most intense happiness in its own right. I even hope to persuade you that we can find in our world what I shall call 'our objective redemption'. At last we feel completely at home in the world and can let go. This is *it*, here and now – the wingéd joy, eternity's sunrise.

Note

A student asks: 'Shouldn't you define happiness?' I think he means something like this: the sort of English utilitarian ethics that stems from

Jeremy Bentham and John Stuart Mill sets out to make happiness the supreme principle of morality and the only intrinsic good – but then it runs into the familiar objection that happiness can't be the only good, because it can't exist alone and it can't be pursued 'pure'. Pleasure or happiness is always secondary or consequential. One is not just happy full stop, but happy *because* ... Feelings of pleasure or happiness accompany or colour something else that we are doing or experiencing. So happiness can't quite be pursued directly as an end in itself; it is experienced as a bonus, a by-product, a feeling that we'll have when we have achieved something else.

In reply, I suggest that we turn the problem round, and look at the problem of happiness from the negative and therapeutic side. More, and much more pervasively, than most people realize, we human beings are unhappy for reasons that philosophy can cure. When we have been freed from the errors and blockages that have made us unhappy, happiness will reassert itself spontaneously.

Notice here how we speak of life's joy in its own self-affirmation, and of having a healthy *appetite* for life. I take this to mean that just the passage of time, *feeding* us fresh experiences, is pleasurable. That, at least, is how it should be: we should often *feast* our eyes, *drink in* a sight, and *lap up* what we hear being said. We do well to assume that people should normally *enjoy* life; and if they are not enjoying it we should ask why, and perhaps seek a way of removing whatever is preventing their enjoyment.

2. The last philosophy

Liberal democracy is the politics of ordinariness. It gives priority, as its standard of rationality and good judgment, to the historically-evolved, historically-changing popular consensus that is expressed in ordinary language and ordinary life. It is in a sense the last politics, the End of History, because from now on we will be continually recalling ourselves to it. It is a consensus that keeps on needing to be reappraised, renegotiated.

Similarly, by the last philosophy I mean, not something grand, but something modest. I see it as equivalent to Kingdom-religion: it aims high, it aims for blessedness, but it does so within ordinariness. It requires us to give up the idea of philosophy as a super-science that sets out to give us a peculiarly-complete and

9

morally-neutral summary of the structure of Reality. No, because we need to forget the idea that there is an objective Truth of things, out-there and independent of us and our values. There is no more-real order of things; nothing is deep and there is no Beyond for philosophy to tell us about. A philosophy should instead be seen, more modestly, as being something like a work of art that aims to make it easier for us to follow a certain way of life.

A philosophy, then, is a literary construction, a work of art, a network of unifying and totalizing metaphors that sets out to conjure up a fairly-coherent picture of the world. The world is thus 'envisioned', as the Americans say, as a fit arena for the living of a certain kind of life. Historical examples of the lifestyles towards which philosophies have been geared include the life of philosophical contemplation, the life of strenuous moral action, the life of revolutionary practice, the life of a scientist, the life of a creative artist, the life of an aesthete, and so on.

When I use the phrase 'the last philosophy', I do not of course intend it in anything like the Nietzschean sense. Although Plato and Nietzsche stand at opposite ends and opposite poles of the Western philosophical tradition, they were both of them bloodcurdlingly élitist. Only *after* Nietzsche does philosophy at last get to be decently democratic. This can happen as and when philosophy becomes completely naturalistic. All thought of a Higher World and of a superior order of things to which some superior class of human beings have access is given up. Everything returns into the here and now, into ordinariness, into mundanity, into transience and relativity.

The last philosophy, then, takes the form of a democratic metaphysics of ordinary life. To achieve this, we must above all else overcome the doctrine of what Leibniz called 'metaphysical evil'. This is the doctrine that the whole of our human condition is, in a non-culpable and structural way, blighted. We just can't be wholly happy, because we are structurally subject to finitude, and therefore to limitation, time, corruption, transience – in short, to imperfection. A radical unsatisfactoriness, we are told, pervades the whole of our life in this world. Then we start to think of ourselves as exiled from a better world that is not blighted like this one; and so we fall into the power of various sorts of expert who propose to tell us about that better world, guide us to it and, in the meanwhile, rule over us in its name.

The last philosophy, in the sense of a democratic metaphysics of ordinary life, attempts to liberate people from the belief that there is something structurally wrong with this life of ours. Recognizing as we must that this life is the last life we'll ever live, these bodies are the last bodies we'll ever have, and this world is the last world we will ever know, the last philosophy seeks to persuade people that there's nothing structurally wrong with the human condition. Because the human condition is outsideless, there is nothing beyond it to which it is in any way inferior or for which it is only a preparation. We can live without the sense that we are in a state of exile. We can live without the idea of a better world than this, and without those old experts. Where we are is 'ultimate reality' – a silly phrase. This life has no Beyond: it's final and it's just fine. And because of the theological background out of which I have come to this point, it must be clear that the last philosophy is equivalent to a Kingdom-theology: the point being that both philosophers and theologians have at last come to a time when they can drop the idea that their prime task is to justify somebody else's authority over us during a difficult and un-satisfactory period of transition. We are no longer in transition: we are *there*. We have arrived at our final destination. The world is, in a very strong sense, *our* world, our home.

So you can view this book as a work either of democratic philosophy or of Kingdom-theology. What links the two descrip-tions is the way I here try to show that perfect *religious* happiness is possible here and now. We have no need to feel in any way alienated, because the mind, language and the objective world are all made of one and the same continuous stuff. We should not experience our own transience as distressing: we should be easy, going. Our life is endless, because of the way we are wholly woven into and a part of the endless flux of things. I want you to feel an intense joy in life, joy in sunshine. I'm offering an interpretation of the Apostle's jubilant cry that 'All things are yours'. I'm thus attempting to deliver heaven on earth – or to show that Earth is already Heaven – which makes this a piece of religious writing. It offers our final happiness, and therefore (paradoxically) final deliverance from religion as it has been hitherto understood.

Note

Some people have objected that what I am calling democratic philosophy or 'Kingdom-theology' is over-optimistic. But I am saying simply that we now have very strong reasons for giving up the idea that this life is merely transitional or preparatory; and therefore we should criticize and try to update all those institutions which justify their authority over us by telling us that they are training and disciplining us in preparation for another world yet to come. (Morality is a case in point.) I *am* denying 'metaphysical evil': I am of course not denying the familiar facts of 'moral evil' (human sin or wickedness) and 'natural evil' (pain and suffering). But I am insisting that giving up the idea of metaphysical evil makes a startlingly big difference, by helping us at last to feel fully at home in our own world.

3. What is life?

'That's life', 'Life's like that'. But what is *life*? A strange, almost a cosmic word, for we use it to invoke the whole span and the whole world of human existence, the only world that actually presents itself. It is temporal and processual, a continuously outpouring and self-renewing Now, as still as a fountain. There are no gaps in it. It emerges, it pours out, so that Martin Heidegger has called it E-vent, outcoming. He wants to equate Being with the continual emergence or present-ing of the world of Becoming. But in this discussion let us forget the talk of Being. Let us forget the whole wearisome, misleading vocabulary of existence and substance, and stick to the word *life*. It has several advantages. It reminds us that an organism's biological life is indeed a continuous motion without any interruption between birth and death, that its life is maintained by its own appetite for life, and that its life is a continual process of exchange with its environment. It has to have a world, an environment which it is both drawing upon and producing all the time, non-stop.

So let us say simply that it is the world of our human life that presents itself: and that contrary to the impression given by the immense variety of philosophies, religions and other systems of thought, nobody ever has lived or ever will live anywhere else but in all this. Our only known home is this milieu which we call Life.

This is *it* – the E-ventuating *now*, outpouring, uninterrupted, a life-world maintained by its own appetite for itself, and in a condition of continual exchange, both amongst living things and between them and their environment. The exchange is both physical (an exchange of energies and chemicals) and cultural (an exchange of signs, communication); and the environment is something that the organism both produces and is produced by. We receive and send, make and are made.

Now we take a few steps back, to a point before the organism has differentiated itself either from other organisms or from the environment. As an exercise, lie in bed tonight in the darkness and silence. Reduce all external stimuli to the minimum, but remain alert and attentive until you can hear first the beating of your own heart and then in time the slow surgings of the rest of your physiology. That's life. Now wait and listen out for the E-vent, the forthcoming of Becoming. You are acutely conscious, with open eyes, but you are not at all *self*-conscious. You are indeed undistracted by thoughts of the self or by awareness of any boundary between the self and the not-self. You don't make, and you don't feel, the dubious distinction between inner and outer. You are just alertness and attentiveness, floating back as close as you can get to the forthcoming or E-ventuation of life.

What presents itself? A dark, turbid flux of upwelling, tangled energies. Because it can't present itself to awareness *at all* unless it has already been at least partly formed and lit up by language, it is to some extent already a train of thought, a stream of consciousness, the brain's logorrhea, life's slightly delirious struggling forth into expression.

So here you rest at the origin of all things, where (as the old mythologies say) the upwelling primal Chaos emerges into the light as it gets formed by language. You are such a languagey being that in you the very forthcoming of Becoming is already formed and facilitated by language.

The next point here is perhaps best made in erotic terms. Eros as a drive can emerge only in so far as it finds an object-form that draws it out. It needs to be aroused. When you know what you want, you know what you're 'into'. The form of the desired object awakens desire. Desire rushes into it, filling it and being formed by it. Similarly, the ceaseless activity of the language-generating area of the brain proffers possible forms for Chaos to come forward into.

> D.C. Dennett and other writers on consciousness claim that the brain is constantly formulating, trying out and revising hypotheses. This is too complimentary, picturing 'the brain' as a scientist, and forgetting the question of language. What really happens, as I have said, is that the language-generating area of the brain churns out words and phrases very rapidly. The ones to which 'affect' or 'life-energy' attaches itself come forward into illuminated consciousness for more leisurely entertainment (Williams James' discussion – 'The Sentiment of Rationality' – is, as usual, pretty good here.) It is worth adding that the language-generator can learn by experience which words and phrases stand the best chance of being gratifyingly filled as they 'come to mind'. This shortens the search-process greatly.

And that is why, as you lie quietly and attentively in the darkness, trying to watch the continual emergence of Becoming, what you will observe coming forth is a flux that is already at-least-partly lit up by language. It has had to take on a bit of shape, both semantic (to give it form) and syntactic (to give it continuity), in order to be able to emerge at all. Which is why the creation out of Chaos described in *Genesis* was in due course redescribed by the church as creation out of nothing – creation without *anything* being real prior to the utterance of the life-giving Word. And just as Eros comes to life when the form of the desired awakens desire, so the flux of becoming E-ventuates, comes to be, comes to life, as it finds forms to come out into. The featherlight dance of words calls desire, the energies of life, forth into Becoming.

Beware at this point of the temptation to equate Chaos with the Unconscious. In so far as there are conflicting forces within your make-up, they will show up in the language you produce. So the Conscious/Unconscious distinction is the same as that between text and subtext; that is, it is a distinction that can be made *within* the language and body-language that appears and moves on your surface. Remember, the *Un*conscious is already linguistic, already formed by culture. When in our nocturnal meditation we were listening intently, we were *not* trying to listen to the psychologically Conscious emerging from the Unconscious. Certainly not: that is not at all what we were listening out for. We were listening to the Now renewing itself. We were listening to the E-ventuation of Becoming, the steady coming-forth of the world from moment to moment.

So perhaps the meditation will not be done rightly or profitably unless and until you have been convinced by the later arguments in this book by means of which I try to get rid of the thing that is called 'the mind', conscious and unconscious. Get rid of that inner space or ghost within, get rid of the biological-drives view of the Unconscious, and then it will become much easier to hear the world *coming to life*, creating itself.

This is the first and neatest example of the way bad philosophy cuts us off from the procession or coming-forth of Becoming, the source of our life.

In the exercise just performed we went as far back towards the source of our life as it is possible to go. We did the philosophical equivalent of saying our prayers, resting in the sort of state which religion calls 'silent regard', or 'mindfulness'. Now repeat the exercise, but in a slightly more wakeful and energized state of consciousness, a bit like lucid dreaming perhaps: at any rate, with a noticeably stronger illumination of the scene. What shows up?

This time, life presents itself as a stream of experience, activity and consciousness. Watch it go by: that's experience. Stand in the midst of it, letting it pass by and through you in such a way that your own idiosyncrasy deflects it a bit, this way or that: that is action. And the irregular flickering that illuminates the scene: that's consciousness.

We are still not making that old pernicious inner/outer distinction. Notice that the contrast between what's real, out-there, and what's 'only in your mind' is a highly objectionable distinction, because it makes everybody's 'mind' a place of illusion and unreality in which the individual is locked up in solitary confinement. That's foul. So forget it: unmake that prison. *Consciousness*, the brightness, the seen-ness, the heard-ness, the known-ness of the world, is all out there in the public realm. Your subjective consciousness is not something distinct and interior: it is your access to and your participation in the brightness of the common public world. Consciousness is not inside; it's out in front. Look at the objects before you, in your visual field. At this moment I see a red ballpoint pen, my bunch of keys, the brown wooden surface of the desk – and my consciousness of these things is not situated inside my eye-sockets or my visual cortex. It is objective. I see them bright, out-there. It is precisely by spreading our consciousness of things and our valuations of them over them, out-there, and by doing it in a way governed by common rules, that we together constitute a common life-world. Correction: *our* common life-world. So if you were to join me you'd see just the same pen, keys and desk. We'd be *con-skious*, co-knowing the very same things, in such a way as to share the same consciousness. As people rightly put it, we talk the same language, see things the same way, have things in common, and live in the same world. (My allegedly rarefied philosophy merely draws attention to well-tried phrases in ordinary everyday language. I'm telling you only things you already know: that's what I mean by a democratic metaphysics of ordinariness. I'm not trying to sell you anything; I'm only trying to show you that you are fine as you are. No news is good news, so my evangel is that there is no news.)

Let's pursue now the question of consciousness, resuming our meditation and trying to attend very quietly to the way in which biological urges, running words, and consciousness are related to each other. Once again, it's all there, if we will but attend to it.

What then is consciousness? It arises in so far as bits of the flux of things, as they come streaming forth, take on form or structure. Where a strand in the flux becomes sign-formed or (more specifically) language-formed, it becomes illuminated. It starts to shine, it becomes conscious, intelligible. Obscurely, and somewhat paradoxically, we may sense, in the surging painful disorder of our most violent and inarticulate feelings, what the world might be like if there were no language. Darkness, blind Chaos. But these too are words: 'inarticulate' articulates! It is too paradoxical to pretend to be able to represent how things were prior to there being any representation of them. A world not yet represented is not even 'a world'.

So what presents itself to the meditator is always already our human life, a forthcoming continuous flux of energies that is already partly lit up by language. (The illumination is so far only partial, because the signs that have so far engaged with the flux are relatively few and general.) But exactly how does language illuminate Chaos, making biological processes conscious? Think slow, watch. In the first place, the sign is general. When an event in the flux becomes sign-formed, put into words, the generality of the sign creates allusions and crosslinks to other events elsewhere in the flux, past or future, actual or possible. This begins to organize the flux, pushing up out of it an ideal observer or 'reader' of it who is set back a little and is no longer immersed in pure immediacy. Only an ideal observer, of course; but the present argument is that the generality of the sign and the great associative or 'disseminative' activity of words means that as soon as the sign hits the flux it creates ripples, allusions, associations, trains of thought, sparks. Language starts to run faster, and feelings start to bubble. Things brighten up. That's consciousness, and I call it *phosphorescence*, a lighting-up of the flux.

Watch while you meditate or daydream. We tend to speak of consciousness as a spotlight, falling upon and illuminating one area or another of our dark, turbid emergent brain-activity, and perhaps lighting it up as conscious, articulate thought. But the metaphorical *falling* of the light should be erased. There is no homunculus, or little man, in your head watching your brain activity. There is no subject of consciousness, holding a torch and directing a beam of light. Cut him out and speak instead of the light as *given off* like phosphorescence; or think of it as sparking. Consciousness is an effect of the very rapid, only half-articulated motion of language in our systems, drawing out and forming desire, making a world.

A long history of matter-mind dualism has left us with the notion that consciousness is something simple, unique and irreducible. But is it? Ask yourself what is the difference between the way a video-camera sees something and the way you see something. Isn't the answer that, unlike the camera, you can actually *tell* what it is that you see? That is, you can discriminate and describe what is before you. You can put it all into words. My feeling that I am conscious is the feeling that, unlike a mere camera, I am a speaker, I have a world in which I belong with others. I am a witness because I can *bear* witness; I can *tell* what I see.

Thus it would be better for us not to speak of consciousness as a unique spiritual quality that is superadded to certain very complex physical systems. Instead it would be better and simpler for us to view consciousness as confidence in one's capacity to speak and thereby to build with others a common world. Consciousness equals articulacy.

Notice especially that consciousness is not something inward and hidden, like dreaming or fantasy. On the contrary, I know I'm conscious now because I'm sure that I'm using the public language and I'm in the public world. The sanity and clarity of my consciousness depends upon the strength and clarity of the public world before me, in which I know I am situated, and of which I know I can speak.

This brings us to a second point about language and how it gets into our systems, because I have been reminding you of various metaphors of physical – not to say, sexual – contact between human bodies, metaphors of warmth, chemistry, friction, electricity and sparking. Why? It's like this: intensely social creatures, we've got to get along together. We've got to communicate, making gestures, noises and marks by means of which we adjust to each other and co-operate with each other. In many and various ways we square up to each other, negotiate, fence and haggle with, woo, serve, threaten, thank and greet each other, and so on; and all this requires communication, which requires signs, which, again, require a little pressure – which in turn creates a little 'sparking' or 'electricity'. What happens is that the motion of signs on *your* surface makes *mine* tingle. A few signs rub off you and on to me, with an effect like the crackling of static electricity. Contact raises consciousness; and the daily pressure of one life against another is managed by being ritualized. By signing to each other, we acknowledge each other, and this mutual acknowledgment is coded into standard, familiar signs, routines, forms of exchange and language-games. I'm using the usual bullshitting academic jargon, but the philosophical point is made perfectly clearly by everyday idioms: when you lean on me, if it is

18

clear what game you're playing I'll be able to get your message. Especially in some middle-class Protestant circles, there is a tendency to speak disparagingly of rituals. But that is a mistake, because ritualization creates intelligibility. Without it – without, that is, the differentiation of a very large number of distinct language-games and standard forms of utterance – we would not have been able to develop language, social life and a common world at all. We'd still be clashing by night, in the dark.

To recapitulate: turning up the light and coming forward a little towards individual consciousness and activity, we have seen that the dark flux of life presents itself always as already *human* life, called forth into Becoming, lit up and formed by language, and seen as if by an ideal observer who is just a little raised out of the flux. All this can be verified personally by anyone who quietly reflects and watches the process of her or his own thinking. Try, for example, to think a wordless thought. I do so. I hear the *Brm* of traffic, of a motorbike, outside – but that is to say that those words enabled me to hear something as I listened. The words provided forms, and noise E-vented as sound, the sound of a motorbike. Brm, Brm. Kant says that objective empirical know-ledge begins when intuition and concept click together. The intuition is the raw datum of experience; the concept is the mental form. What we are finding stands in that tradition, but notice the all-important differences. Kant calls the world of Becoming the 'phenomenal' world, the apparent world; we call it the life-world. Kant makes the traditional matter-form distinction, talking of how sense-intuitions are formed by concepts. We find that the raw material of the life-world is a dark turbid flux of energies, which are called forth into Becoming, lit up and formed, by language.

How does all this happen? We have seen so far that it happens in the first place because the sign is general, and in the second place because the sign is interactive or social. Signs and sign-systems, rituals and language-games, are evolved where one complex organism rubs up against another and where they really need to do business with each other. And now, in the third place, as we begin to understand each other's body-language (*all* language being body-language, of course), as signs get arranged in sequences and exchanges become ritualized, proper syntactically-ordered language becomes a force that does *work*. It develops the relationship between the sender and the receiver. They become more aware of each other and, reflexively, of themselves. Reciprocal pressure creates a little prickling, electricity, phosphorescence, consciousness. They each become aware of the way in which the idiosyncrasy of an individual's physical system comes out into expression in her or his communication. We'll not succeed in communicating at all, unless our linguistic behaviour is very highly disciplined and rule-governed. But every performance is also an interpretation, and even if every single thing we say and do is conventional and follows some prescribed form, a touch of personal peculiarity will always come through.

At the beginning of this section we asked, 'What is life?'. Kant would not have raised such a question. In his day philosophers were above all impressed by mathematical physics, the first really successful science. By applying *a priori* mathematical principles to the local motions of material bodies, Newton had gone most of the way to constructing a complete fundamental science of nature. An extraordinary achievement, so great that it seemed to deserve a central place in philosophy. How had it been possible; and how were humanity's other major concerns to be rethought in the light of it? Such was Kant's 'problematic'.

The agenda has now been rewritten, principally by Darwin. That's why we begin by asking, 'What is *life*?'. Since antiquity human beings have seen themselves as somehow transcending the world of mere Nature. The ploughman who made oxen labour for him, the nun in her convent and the bronze equestrian statue of a king, all spoke of the human will to rule Nature. But I am saying that after Darwin we couldn't help but come to see that our whole existence is intra-biological. We are always inside our life, and we know of no other angle on the world. For us, our life-world is *the* world. What we are, what we've got, how we tick, is all there is.

It is easy to see from this why the medical profession has become so important in modern times, but of more immediate concern to us now is the new philosophical agenda. What is life, indeed? How have we animals become humans, how has culture emerged from nature, and how in particular have we learnt to speak? How has the world of biological feeling, of stimulus and response, become the world of cultural meanings, the world of words and of consciousness?

How then, from a radically intra-biological starting-point, are we to explain language, thought, and our construction of the social and physical worlds? And when we have those questions sorted out, we can re-open the old questions about the Good: about our values, and about what sort and degree of happiness may be accessible to us.

Notes

Philosophy is an activity, but there are not many books that expressly set out to teach the reader how to do it. Descartes pretends to be setting us Jesuit-style spiritual exercises to be followed one a day for a week; but does anybody actually philosophize like that? Many other philosophers have given glimpses here and there of themselves at work, and the student gratefully seizes upon these; but most philosophy is highly literary, and all-too-careful to conceal its own character as text and the process by which it came into being.

Accordingly, in this book I have included near the beginning an account of how you can learn to philosophize, and an illustration of how I do it; but more than that, I have in effect claimed that the medium and the message are here one and the same. Admittedly, a philosophy-book is only a string of words, marks on paper. But in the body of the book (and in too many books, written over too many years) I have argued that language is ubiquitous, language covers over and forms everything, and language goes all the way back to the beginning. Accordingly I have in this section just completed included a brief account of how you too can go back to the beginning of all things and verify the book's central theses for yourself. Check me out by going back to the place from which these words come – from which, indeed, all words come. If you find I'm right, then philosophy is possible.

I've made elsewhere some provocative remarks about the difficulty of writing a religious book which is not an attempt to deceive and manipulate the reader. But it is equally difficult to find a philosophy book that is candid about its own possibility-conditions and the machinery by which it was actually produced. The reason for the difficulty, in the case of philosophy, is that unless language itself already goes all the way back to the beginning of things, and already covers everything from every angle, one cannot hope to write a philosophy text that does so. But precisely that is my doctrine, so I *can* hope. Philosophy does aim at a very special kind of completeness, in such a way that a philosophy-book has not earned the name of philosophy unless its medium is fully consistent with its message, and the text must include a transparent account of its own possibility-conditions and its own genesis as text. So I'm telling you: I went back to the beginning, there I found that there was already language, and I made all this up – or rather, it made itself up. I report what is there *in* the very stuff I found there. Check out these claims – and then consider their implications. The loopy, 'extreme' doctrines here put forward are no more than the possibility-conditions for philosophy as a subject. There's method in my madness.

The argument just put forward is, you'll see, a philosophical version of the old belief – referred to again below – that the scriptural text is pre-existent in eternity. Scripture says it all, and can do so because it goes back to the very beginning. Go back yourself and listen to the language-generator; you'll hear it saying everything there is to be said. The beginning of the world and the meaning of it all is all whirring away in your brain *already*. I'm not taking you anywhere else: I'm only asking you to listen to where you already are.

Philosophers and texts of value in teaching one how to philosophize include (I'd say) Plato, Berkeley's notebooks, Hume's *Treatise*, Kierkegaard's journals and papers, Nietzsche's literary remains. Wittgenstein? – Not quite, somehow, perhaps because he was, alas, always hiding something. Heidegger's late work? – Somehow, Yes.

'Lucid dreaming', by the way, is the sort of half-awake dreaming in which we seem to ourselves to be able to control the course of the dream-events.

A friendly critic points out the paradox lurking in my project of a democratic metaphysics of ordinary life and ordinary language, purporting to convey the good news that there is no news. Why bother? Why take the trouble to say what doesn't need saying? Philosophy, surely, must claim to have something to tell us: one cannot even say that there is no secret without somehow making 'There is no secret' into a new form of secret knowledge.

Wittgenstein would answer, surely, that many or most people are still caught up in various philosophical illusions and misleading pictures left over from the past. It is a great relief to be delivered from them. I want to add that in our own noisy and overcrowded culture one can very easily lose sight of ordinariness. And in particular, I want to show the reader various things that we can't see because they are too close to us.

4. On what there is

The philosophical doctrine I am propounding is very simple. It is that we do best to picture the world as a beginningless, endless and outsideless stream of language-formed events that continually pours forth and passes away.

The stream of events is dense and many-stranded. One strand in it is this chain of graphic signs which you are now perusing. (Or, if you happen to be hearing this read aloud, the series of honks-and-barks-heard-as-signs to which you are now listening.) This has the happy consequence that in our philosophy the medium is a bit of the message it conveys. By that I mean that the medium in which I speak is entirely of a piece with the stuff about which I speak, which explains how this one strand is able to represent the whole. What there is is lots and lots more of *this*, stuff like what's going on here and now.

You may think that the doctrine sounds familiar. It seems to resemble phenomenalism, Mahayana Buddhism, Russell's neutral monism and William James' radical empiricism, all of which see the world as a flux of tiny events, scraps of experience. However, the world of a living being cannot be made of atoms with voids between, chiefly because biological life has to be a continuous flowing process. It cannot tolerate being interrupted by voids. So like James we portray the flux as being made not only of elements but also of relations between them, joining them up; but unlike James we say expressly that it is language that joins events up and so gives to the world its flowing temporal continuity. In the world of signs, one thing leads to another and so on indefinitely. That, surely, anyone will acknowledge. And in the world of thought it is also easy to see that it is language that gives to thought its endless, *perpetuum mobile*, running or current character. Similarly, in 'the world' in the philosophical sense, the world of events, anything may be a sign, and has to be recognized as a sign in order to be got hold of, in order to become determinate, intelligible and so apprehensible. In order to present itself, our world – and we can know of no other world than ours – must present iself as being always already sign-formed.

In Greek philosophy, things needed to be Formed in order to be real enough to be thinkable; and in Kant's philosophy the manifold of intuition (that is, raw sense-experience) has to be formed by concepts in order to become object-ive and intelligible. So, where the Greeks put their Forms and Kant put his concepts, I'm putting just words, with the advantage that as I insist that our world is always already formed by our language so I'm also claiming that our world is thereby constituted as a flowing temporal world, a *life*-world. So it is that we enact the unity of life and language, the flesh and the word, life-time and world-time. Have we yet considered all the implications of the thought that our first clock was the one we have in the base of the brain? The original pace-setter, the lifetimepiece.

The stream of events is prior to the making of any distinction between the world of subjective experience on the one hand and the public, social world on the other. So we should say here that, being many-stranded, the stream of events is legible in many different ways, and with different interests in mind. Read with an interest in *subjectivity*, it is read as the world of experience, the world of thought, the world as seen from *my* point of view, foregrounding my own wishes, hopes and fears. Read in the vocabulary of ordinary language, with an interest in the physical and social worlds around us, it is seen as the objective public world, the *Lebenswelt*. Read mathematically, it becomes the world of mathematical physics. Here, however – and rather more strongly than in *After All* – I have argued for giving a very special place to a biological reading of the stream of events, and to a biological thought-experiment. The reason I have been offering for this rather unusual prioritizing of biology is that we nowadays have very strong reasons for thinking that no non-biological being has – or has ever had – a world at all. The only eyes that have ever looked upon a world, and indeed the only eyes *period* are the eyes of animals like ourselves. So it is worth giving a special place to biology: the ambient world just has to be life-like.

Ancient philosophy began – in Greece at least – by searching for an *archē* or First Principle of all things. That enquiry now appears to have been a mistake, which is why the sentence in which I stated my doctrine claimed only that we would 'do best to picture the world' thus and so. The world of philosophy has no *archē*, just as the world of signs has no *archē*.

The reason for my recommendation is that from this starting point – i.e., the world as 'a beginningless, endless and outsideless stream of language-formed events', as illustrated by the thought-experiment described in Section 3 – we can quickly get to all other places on the map of culture. So my one-sentence metaphysics merely describes the cross-roads at the centre of the town; and no more than that. We cannot trace the structure of reality any further back than the structure of the various languages (natural, mathematical, musical, etc.) in which it must present itself.

Notes

Very few philosophers have had any proper qualifications in biology, but Locke and James were doctors of medicine. A few further philosophers show some real sympathy with biology: Schopenhauer, Nietzsche, Bergson, Whitehead and Deleuze.

For various historical reasons, many modern philosophers have held that no secure starting-point or foundation for metaphysics can be found which does not generate paradoxes. See, for example, Hilary Lawson, *Reflexivity* (Hutchinson 1985). My opening paragraphs, if read aloud, sidestep the difficulty by simultaneously saying and showing and being a sample of what there is, and indeed of *all* that there is. There is *this* – a language-formed discharge of energies, pouring forth and passing away.

Stephen Pinker, in *The Language Instinct* (Allen Lane: The Penguin Press, 1994), evidently thinks that armchair philosophy-of-language has now been made obsolete by the very rapid development of new empirical sciences of cognition and language.

One can see what he means; but there is still a place for philosophy to make its special contribution. For just look at the way Pinker's text assumes scientific realism, and constantly makes internally the distinction between language and non-language. Suppose that a painter were similarly confident that just on the painted surface – just in paint – he could mark out the distinction between the visible and the invisible: wouldn't Pinker feel this a bit puzzling?

I agree that philosophy often nowadays looks as if it is on the brink of becoming redundant and vanishing as a subject. Nevertheless, I am trying to show that there remains something very important that philosophy is; something that must on no account become lost and forgotten.

Science brackets-out the observer, makes him merely 'ideal'. Philosophy, I am saying, tries for a special kind of all-round completeness by including us and our own interests, *and even its own production as text*, within its own vision of the world. Try reading the opening sentences of Section 4 *aloud*.

5. The natural history of reason

Remember, nothing is logically prior to language. Trying to think outside language and our human life-world is rather like trying to think outside one's own life. One cannot avoid continuing to presuppose the very thing that one is pretending to have left behind.

Imagine, for example, that you are one of those misunderstood teenagers who thinks: 'I wish I were dead. They'll be sorry when I'm gone.' And you start to imagine the scene: you see your own lifeless corpse, and your remorseful parents shedding a tear or two over it. But of course you are still there, hovering invisibly, observing this touching scene and getting a whole lot of posthumous satisfaction from it. So you haven't really thought your own death at all. What's more, all thought about life after death makes the same error. From which the proper conclusion to draw is that we should forget about 'subjective immortality', because for each individual subject the world is exactly as long and as large as the span and the scope of his or her life. From the subjective point of view our life is finite but outsideless, and death should be forgotten. On this point Spinoza was correct (*Ethics* IV, Prop. LXVII).

Before we leave this example we should recall, of course, that although each individual subject dies, the public social realm continues. Provisions made by an individual before his own death may continue to have effects in the public realm after his death; and to that extent we are of course able to think about life (i.e., other people's lives) after our death. We remember our own dead kinsfolk, and may hope in due course to be similarly remembered ourselves. That is 'objective immortality'.

The immediate point, however, is that there is a paradox in any attempt to think subjective immortality. And there is a similar paradox in any attempt to think outside language. Just as, in the case of death, we imagined ourselves still being around so that we could watch people feeling dreadfully guilty about not having treated us more kindly, whilst we were still alive ('But now it's too *late*, boo hoo!'), so too in the case of language, when we try to think beyond language we have of course surreptitiously smuggled it along with us in order to do so. To think beyond language, one needs language.

I will readily allow that for some purposes, and in certain areas, we do and we must conjure up within language accounts of things and states of affairs that we have reason to postulate as existing or having existed seemingly beyond the scope of language. But in such a case – as when a physicist in a work of popular science describes the Big Bang – it is important to remind the audience that one is telling a Just-So story from an impossible standpoint, about an event that *ex hypothesi* nobody could have attended or described. Without such a reminder, scientific theory is understood too 'realistically' and turns into a new, mystifying and highly-objectionable mythology. As, of course, has already happened.

All that is by the way. Our present concern is simply to reiterate the primacy of ordinary language and the life-world. Any attempt to give something else priority will only take us back into mystification and alien domination. That is why I insist upon the primacy of the life-world and ordinary language: just for political reasons, epistemological democracy is to be preferred. It is saner. There will no doubt always be people who claim to have privileged knowledge of a superior realm outside the sphere of ordinary language and everyday life. Such people have included, in particular, priests, philosophers and scientists. They always claim that if only they were in charge they'd be able to show us how to make a better fist of everyday life than we are doing at present. They claim that their expert knowledge of a secondary world – which may be the world of the gods, the world of necessary truth or the world of scientific theory – qualifies them to tell us how we should live in the world of ordinary language and everyday life.

History, unfortunately, does not lend much credence to their claim (I dare to say this because I am or have been all three myself, and have found that I'm no expert). Of course we may and we do consult them in certain tight spots, but what they should *not* be allowed to do is displace ordinary language and everyday life from its metaphysical priority as the ultimate reference-point for determining questions about meaning, truth and values. By the end of the twentieth century we've had a bellyfull of think-tanks, ideologues, fanatics, nostrums, gurus, panaceas, experts. After all that, don't we circle back with a sense of relief to Wittgenstein's view that sanity lies in ordinariness?

What instinct prompts us to think, argument confirms. For the priest, the philosopher and the scientist had to become human beings before ever they could become specialized professionals, and even as they use their specialized vocabularies they cannot help referring back all the time to ordinary language and everyday life as 'the prime analogate', the benchmark, the anchor, the norm, the reference-point that must always be presupposed in order to give meaning to what they say. All words, metaphors and usages need to keep a thread running back to some everyday usage which is their primary 'site', from which they draw their meaning. Unless the specialized professional thus tacitly recognizes and acknowledges the primacy of the everyday, what he or she says becomes so much hot air. It floats away, useless; it has no grip on anything.

Think of the way in which all the technical terms of any branch of knowledge are compound words, whose Greek or Latin roots run back into the concrete and the everyday; don't we see here how the key insight of British Empiricism can be saved, and is correct, provided only that it is re-expressed in linguistic terms? The home ground or 'primary site' of all meaning, to which we must refer in order to check out the cash-value of large and general statements, is not simple sense-experience, but the language-games of ordinary people and ordinary life.

So the professionals cannot be allowed to get away with their old trick of concealing their own necessary grounding in everydayness – and therefore their own secondariness – in order to claim the right to lord it over us. No – and the point here is one that David Hume, in his way, grasped long ago – given *their own dependence upon* everyday language and everyday life, they cannot enter our everyday world as if from above, claiming to possess supermundane authority, fresh information, fresh promises and threats; claiming in effect that the everyday realm is *dependent upon them*. Nonsense: for if there is anything that stands upon its own feet, it is everydayness. Everything else is derivative, including all expertise.

Certainly we may consult the experts as professional advisers, and there are many circumstances in which they can be of help to us. But they cannot justify their historic claims to lord it over us, and it is right to insist that while they are our valued servants and counsellors, they should not become our masters.

Obviously enough, all these considerations apply also to reason itself. We smiled at the naiveté of a person who tries to imagine her state after her own death, or who tries to think outside language; and by the same token we have to forget the old belief that there is an Order of Reason, a world of eternal truths and intelligible essences prior to and independent of human language. Nobody ever met or will meet such a doctrine except, of course, *within* a human language. We should therefore naturalize reason, and see the whole *a priori* realm as stating the conditions for the establishment of language as a, no, *the* social institution, and its successful use thereafter. Jaw-jaw will not become established as an improvement upon war-war unless it is biologically advantageous, quicker and more efficient. All the way along it turns out, not surprisingly, that language cannot be thought of as ever having got going in the first place, and cannot be used effectively, without a whole lot of strong antecedent presumptions in favour of consistency, good faith, reliability and the due observance of the rules of the game.

That's reason, and it is entirely immanent. It's a lot of conventions that we have found we must work with: indeed, it's clear on reflection that we just can't imagine how we could do without them. Furthermore, the huge elaboration of the specialized knowledge systems of mathematics and the natural sciences owes its success, not to the introduction of any additional principles of logic, but only to a more systematic and rigorous application of the principles already presupposed by the successful use of language in the simplest linguistic exchanges of everyday life. Wayward but highly social beings, we urgently need to co-operate. We pressurize each other to be reliable, a reciprocal pressure that makes rule-following rational consistency socially imperative. That's reason, and what's wrong with it?

Richard Rorty has said – rightly, I think – that naturalism is the doctrine that everything is contingent. Accordingly, my only defence of my naturalized, pragmatic sort of rationality is that it is just what has been found to work best.

Nothing is prior to language, and nothing is more sacred and primal than simple everydayness. Can I persuade you to share for a moment my astonishment at this thought: that the holy place where Reason springs forth, all meanings are determined, and the world is made – is simply the world of everyday life? The patch of dry land, the primal Mound, the place of creation, the mythic Centre, is ordinariness. Have a nice day.

6. What are words?

Being ubiquitous, like time or the atmosphere, language is extraordinarily difficult to see and to concentrate upon. One has to make the most of such occasional vivid glimpses of it as one may get – perhaps indirectly, or perhaps with the help of a powerful metaphor.

Thus Wittgenstein during the First World War was led by a technical diagram to think that the chief job of a true sentence must be to picture or represent, in a stylized way, the structure of a state of affairs in the world. A true sentence, he thought, is a sort of diagram of a fact. But some fifteen years later, when he was watching hockey or football on Parker's Piece, Cambridge,

Wittgenstein was struck by the very different thought that we *play games* with language – and the metaphor (though often misapplied) has proved powerful and illuminating.

These two metaphors suggest very different views of what language is for. The diagram metaphor suggests that words stand for things, that sentences signify extra-linguistic states of affairs, and that a big text-book is like an atlas of some region of the world. But the game-metaphor suggests that our chief concern is always with other human beings, and that we use language in playing the various games through which we manage our social relationships. Consider how language teachers talk of 'situations', such as greeting, paying a bus fare, shopping, or ordering a meal: knowing a language is a matter of possessing the social skills involved in playing one's part in such everyday-life situations.

Then what is it to *understand* a language? I have described elsewhere a philosophical revelation that occurred in 1984 when two people walked past me talking animatedly in an Asian language. I was struck by the thought that I could hear everything that was being said, and could even guess what was being said – but could understand not a word. So what extra capacity might understanding the meanings of all the words consist in? I mean, I really could hear everything. The speakers were Indo-Europeans – perhaps Bengalis – and therefore not very remote from me culturally. From their intonation and body-language one might guess that they were agreeing vociferously, and no doubt entirely reasonably, in deploring the behaviour of young people or the male sex in general, or even perhaps of some female acquaintance in particular. But what did I lack? Did I need to be carrying with me a portable decoder or translation-machine? Or was it just a matter of social training? I mean, would 'learning to understand their language' simply consist in becoming very much more finely attuned than I was to the nuances of their expressive behaviour?

Two years later, I had a second revelation that took the matter a step further. I lay in a hospital ward at night, having broken some bones. In nearby beds were two old men, both of whom were well on with Alzheimer's. One of them woke suddenly as from a nightmare, and made a series of noises expressive of alarm and expostulation. The other replied with enquiring sounds. The first replied, repeating his fears but in a lower tone, as if recounting them to someone. The second replied again, making calming and reassuring noises – and I began to realize that I was overhearing a wordless conversation that was completely intelligible. Each utterance had, or seemed to have, the shape and sound of an English sentence. After perhaps a dozen of these exchanges the frightened man had been soothed and relaxed. His sounds became fewer, quieter and more hesitant, until both men fell silent and began to breathe regularly once more.

Tennyson speaks of 'An infant crying in the night/And with no language but a cry'. But surely the cries and replies that I had heard *were* language – were, indeed, a complete conversation? I mean, what was missing? Because these two old men were as English as I am, I could not only hear everything they were saying, I could truly understand everything that they said, for I could see that the exchanges between them did the whole of the job that language is by Wittgenstein supposed to do. Their expressive intonation, their coding of feelings into vocal music, was exactly my own, so that my feeling-responses could vibrate exactly in tune with theirs, and I felt that Donald Davidson's celebrated denial of the existence of language must be correct:

> . . . there is no such thing as language, not if a language is anything like what many philosophers and linguists have supposed. There is therefore no such thing to be learned, mastered or born with. We must give up the idea of a clearly defined shared structure which language-users acquire and then apply to cases.
>
> from 'A Nice Derangement of Epitaphs' (in Ernest LePore (ed.), *Truth and Interpretation*, Blackwell 1986, pp. 433–47)

Davidson means to deny structuralist and Chomskyan accounts of language. From his physicalist and expressivist standpoint our words are just noises or marks we've learnt by experience to make by way of seeking the fellow-feeling and co-operation of others, or offering them our own. He objects to the extreme rationalist notion that some deep *a priori* structure has got to be already in place, communally shared and perhaps even genetically encoded, before one person can talk sense to another. And he also objects to the idea that what we mean by what we say, and whether it is true, is decided by its relation to something non-linguistic and quite independent of us.

So I decided that my two old dotards were orthodox Davidsonians, like me. Their noise-making had been a genuine conversation, which made perfectly clear emotional sense and did a good human job. What they'd said was just as good as if it had been said in words. It had even been a genuine English conversation, for I could understand it – indeed, I might in principle have taken part in it, because they and I shared the emotive-expressive phonotaxis of spoken English. They really *were* talking intelligible English! – and all I needed to say about their advanced senility was to suggest charitably that their diction had become very badly slurred. They were still functioning human persons, one consoling the other; much as (or so it is claimed) Willem de Kooning was still a considerable painter, even when he too had advanced Alzheimer's.

Are you ready to accept the idea that our spoken words do not need to be anything more than emotive-expressive noises, conforming to a socially and traditionally-established notation, whereby we communicate with each other to our mutual advantage, getting our feelings and our behaviours into line? We should perhaps add that the precise details of notation, phonotaxis and ritual forms vary from one language-group to another in purely-contingent ways that are for linguists and ethnolinguists, rather than for philosophers, to describe. But that is all we need to add: we shall have fully emancipated ourselves from platonism, and have achieved a genuinely naturalistic view of language, if we are ready to acknowledge that my two dotards had held a genuine English conversation. Words are only the noises we happen to use to do purely human jobs. They don't *need* to have Meanings, if Meanings are supposed to be pure thoughts, intelligible essences. They need only to be expressive noises with conventional uses, through which we are able to get things done.

That said, we need to ask how in that case language ever gets to be descriptive at all. In the course of using language for the purpose of organizing other people, sorting them out, making sure that they think they want to do what we want them to do, voicing our feelings and getting theirs into line, *et cetera*, surely we make a good deal of reference to a common world that we and they inhabit? So how do some of our communicative noises get also to be about a common and public world?

In reply to this question we stress two points. First, living systems are very, very sensitive – so much so that many animal senses are reported in scientific theory to approach the theoretical limits of sensitivity. The creature's olfactory sense can perhaps be switched on by a single molecule of the pheromone, and its visual sense activated by a single photon. This extreme sensitivity – which even we poor humans fully share – makes possible a very, very refined differentiation of our life of feeling, and therefore of our language, and therefore of our world. The world you see in your visual field, before your eyes at this moment, the world of the so-called 'secondary qualities', is the world of your own feeling. Your life of feeling is as differentiated and refined as *that*. Look at it: it's out there in front of you. Your visual field is part, the biggest single part, of your feeling-life.

Or at least, it is of mine: you may be a person of the ear rather than the eye, in which case it will probably be music that above all differentiates, regulates and calibrates the movement of your feelings, and so teaches you to think. It has recently been reported that listening to music enhances people's performance in intelligence tests, and ethnographers have been discussing the idea that a culture's characteristic ways of thinking are coded into its styles in the decorative arts such as textiles, pottery and basketwork. All of which is another indication of the way the old opposition between reason and *aesthesis*, our life of sensuous feeling, is currently breaking down. For is it not the case that the most aesthetically sensitive people – musicians, for example – are usually found to be also the most intelligent?

And now, secondly, we humans in particular, being amongst the most sociable and – especially in our prolonged infancy – the most dependent of all living things, desperately need communication, consensus, co-operation, and above all a common world to live in.

Kant believed that it was pure and universal Reason, working in and through us, that constructs the sensuous world of experience as an ordered objective world. I'm saying he was wrong. It is irrational to believe in objective and universal

Reason. What has given to us our common world is biological, not logical, necessity; our imperative need to construct a common world out of the flux of our feeling-experience. We yearn to be understood. We have to be consistent with each other, and in what we say, or we won't survive: hence reason. It's nothing supernatural: it's a pragmatic necessity.

In summary, what makes reference possible? Answer, our extreme sensitivity, and our desperate need to understand and be understood, have produced a minute differentiation of our feeling-responses and of the words annexed to them. Trading words back and forth, over many, many years, we have gradually built up a common world out of our common language-fixed feelings.

The order we perceive in the objective world reflects the strength of our need for unanimity and our readiness to form and follow conventions. What I see out there is thus not merely the objectification of my own selfhood, but rather the objectification of the *humanum*, the concrete universal human selfhood in which we all live and move and have our being. More of this later.

Note

A student interjects to ask: 'Can one hold a conversation with a pet animal?' On my own account I am bound to answer that we clearly do on occasion communicate – symbolically, emotionally, and even propositionally – with animals and they with us. As you sit in your chair your dog may come up to you carrying your stick, looking hopeful, wagging his tail, making as if to dash off – and you gather that he is saying that he wants to be taken for a walk. On a Davidsonian view of language, it would seem that the dog has indeed said something. For the dog would not be acting so 'transparently' unless on previous occasions it had gone through all this 'performance' and had found that it worked. You got the message; you did as you were asked.

Conversely, a shepherd directing his dog by whistling to it is also surely using a simple language, and to very good effect.

Wittgenstein (*Philosophical Investigations*, 1, 25), discussing all this, says that 'animals simply do not talk'. He seems quite ready to acknowledge that animals like dogs do join us in playing certain very simple language-games. Indeed, that's precisely what we *train* animals to do. But they do not participate in the more complex forms of human language-use. Fair enough: but things have changed somewhat since Wittgenstein's time, chiefly because of the very great and rapid advances in the study of animal behaviour. Nowadays there are dog psychologists who will teach you to read what your dog is saying to you. When he lies very inconveniently in the doorway the dog is bidding for recognition, and when he occupies your chair or your bed he is bidding for leadership. And so on: we are now very good at interpreting what animals are saying: we cover them over with interpretations, we ascribe language to them – and we do it very successfully, which means that we do it rightly.

The effect of this is that the distinctions between language and body-language, and between language and non-language, have become blurred during the past few decades. Here is a new thought: we talking animals have lately got to be so good at talking that we can see talk everywhere. Our theory has become so rich that we've talked the world into being all talk.

Here is another example – it sounds like one of Wittgenstein's – to make the point about language.

'We are putting together a self-assembly wardrobe. You are reading out the assembly instructions and I am screwing the thing together. The noise-gesture for screwing two parts together is the same each time, even when the parts are different. "Screw panel A to panel B" and "Screw panel B to panel C" are gesturally identical. But without a strict system of reference, when A, B and C *stand for* specified components, the assembly language cannot be understood properly, and the wardrobe will not get assembled correctly. From this it seems to follow that language, sometimes at least, operates with a combination of performative speech-act with constitutive reference to some extra-linguistic item, and both are necessary.

'In reply, imagine that as a result of a typing error all the letters designating parts of the wardrobe have been printed as X. You read out: "Screw panel X to panel X". Now although I can't tell exactly what the instruction is, I *can* tell by the noise-gesture that you are speaking a language, and I understand that the speech-act you are using *is* an instruction.

'But now imagine that the opposite printing error has occurred, and that this time the references are printed correctly but the letters of all the other words are replaced by small xs: "xxxxx xxxxx A xx xxxxx B". With the noise-gestures erased, this is no longer recognizable as a language. The point is that noise-gestures and speech-acts *are* necessary for language to be language, but reference isn't.'

So says H. R.-P., whose comments, slightly rewritten by me, I quote with thanks. There is a further point to add, which is made very well by Wittgenstein, Lyotard and others: it is that reference (ostensive definition, nomination, indication) is *itself* taught by speech acts, noise-gestures. So, once again, nothing entirely outside language is necessary for language to be language. Philosophically speaking, all language is in principle like body-language, or like the sign-language used by soldiers in the field, or like the signing of the deaf.

The fullest and most elegant explanation of Wittgenstein's non-realism is that given by D. F. Pears, in *The False Prison: A Study of the Development of Wittgenstein's Philosophy*, two vols, Oxford 1987, 1988.

7. What is thought?

A philosophy book is a very queer sort of book, written under the special constraints that the genre imposes: but within those limits I know what result I want to reach. I want to argue that we human beings can feel completely at home in the world, and have no reason to feel any large-scale or 'cosmic' dissatisfaction with the human condition. We can feel at home for two main reasons: first, because the world is *our* world and, secondly, because everything is made of the same kind of stuff and nothing, therefore, is utterly alien to us.

Both these arguments are counter-intuitive, so I'd better make a very brief apology for each of them.

The claim that the world is *our* world, in a very strong sense, seems counter-intuitive because the top science for almost four centuries has been mathematical physics and because ever since Pascal's time many sensitive souls have felt that the Universe of physics is horribly alien and inhuman. But I've already indicated that physics should no longer dominate philosophy in the way it once did. What now matters most is evolutionary biology. After Darwin, we should be clear that we don't know and never will know any other angle on things than our own. We are biological organisms, and for all intents and purposes our life-world is *the* world, and that's it. And this life-world of ours is always the world of our life, a world structured and coloured by our intense

37

biological interest in life and our symbolic expressions thereof. From square one to square sixty-four (which is death) the world is all ours, our home, full stop. There are no spooks and no mysteries, *none*. Nothing is high and nothing is deep. This world, our life-world, is our only and final home: it has no further world beyond it. It is the world of our own shared feeling, our sympathy: of course it has no Beyond.

The second argument stresses the seamless continuity of this world of ours. Its convincingness will depend especially upon my proving to the general satisfaction that there is no deep and real difference between the allegedly 'internal' world of pure thought and the allegedly 'external' world of physical objects and other people. Everything, including thoughts, material things and language, is made of one sort of stuff which by running everywhere agreeably confuses all distinctions. As Jacques Lacan was perhaps the first to see, no very clear boundary divides the self from its environment. The world, our world, is an endlessly self-renewing continuum in which everything flows into and out of everything else. Me, I *like* having a large penumbra, blurred edges; I *like* containing multitudes.

You may call the metaphysical doctrine I am trying to present 'linguistic naturalism' or 'semiotic materialism', if you like. Bloody jargon. In any case, if I can get you quickly into it, and persuade you that it is in fact what you already think, we can skip the jargon. And the most powerful way in is by the proof of the radical dependence of thought upon language. I have to demonstrate that your supposed inner, private, 'spiritual' world of thought is merely a piece of ideological individualism. It has artificially privatized various things that were originally created in and for the public realm, and ought to remain public.

Again this may seem counter-intuitive (or, in plainer language, contrary to common sense) because in English, Latin and Greek a language is spoken of as a 'tongue' (Latin, *lingua*: Greek, *glossa*). This suggests that language is something produced in the mouth, a mere disposable packaging in which we wrap up our thoughts for transmission to other people. That in turn seems to mean that language is something public, physical and external to the mind. It moves only between us, not inside us.

A philosophical tradition going back to Aristotle suggests that what happens is something like this: we perceive things and form little images of them which are filed away in our memories. Gradually we build up a very large and well-stocked mental model of the world. Thoughts are, as it were, inner pictures or copies of things out there.

How does this happen? The terms used in the Aristotelean tradition seem to suggest that just as I may mould my hand to the shape of an object that I'm picking up, so the mind is made of some kind of ectoplasm or mind-stuff that can conform itself to the shape of any object that it thinks. *Mens est quodammodo omnia*: the mind is in a way all things, endlessly elastic. Thoughts as like little latex mouldings or plaster casts of sense-images. Odd.

However that may be, the classic picture, still reflected in at least some of the things people say, has thought invoking, entertaining, processing and ordering mental images made out of mind-stuff. Some of these images are of particulars; others – general concepts – are more diagrammatic or abstract. The function of words, then, is to stand for or label thoughts. So in my mouth my thoughts get coded into words, and in your ears my words get decoded back into thoughts again.

A corollary of this account is that the world of thought has presumably much the same basic structure for every human being. There is a universal language of pure concepts, 'mentalese', which is used in Heaven, where Dante found that spirits communicate telepathically without the least risk of misunderstanding. Only in the human mouth – so it was believed – has confusion of tongues arisen since Babel. Which brings us to the obvious objection: many idioms in common use surely imply that we think in language? A bilingual person moving to France is aware that within a few days or weeks she is thinking in French, and to prove how deep language goes into personality, a bilingual writer like Samuel Beckett is found to display slightly different literary personalities in different languages. So far from there being any universal language of pure concepts the truth seems rather to be that in different cultures different languages cut up the world in somewhat different ways, and *also* that different languages produce somewhat different subjectivities.

39

Thus ordinary language puzzles us by simultaneously suggesting two very different accounts of what the mind is. One is exalted and even theological, and the other is very homely.

On the exalted account I am a kind of spirit. I occupy and rule over the sub-world of my own inner mental space, very much as God rules over and is omnipresent in the objective world outside. In building my knowledge I construct a replica in my private sub-world of what God has made in the objective world, and I can do this because I am made in God's image and think in something like his way. Thus human knowledge of the world tracks God's creative work, and thinking is a noble spiritual activity.

The homely account is completely different. Long ago I had a friend, a well-known and even episcopal figure called M———, who was very garrulous. We used to speak jocularly of 'the M——— method of arriving at truth', which was to burble on and on and on until he discovered with innocent surprise and satisfaction that he had said something sensible.

I no longer joke about M———. I now think his method of arriving at truth correctly represents the way 'the mind' works. All 'thought' is transacted in signs. That is, it involves an extremely rapid trial-and-error movement of language, which rattles on till something clicks when *le mot juste* comes up. The satisfied click occurs when the feeling that is trying to get expressed finds the form in which it can become articulate. The aim of education is to make the search-process more efficient. As for 'the mind', it is itself a linguistic construct.

I have already given the main arguments for the dependence of thought upon language elsewhere. Here is a brief summary of them.

First, then, historical and biological considerations surely make it clear that unspoken thinking-to-oneself (doing mental arithmetic, for example) must have developed as a privatized, held-back and not-fully-expressed variant of what was originally a public performance. The words were ready for utterance, but then we learned to hold our tongues or bite our lips. At first we were taught to speak, to pray and to calculate out loud, and then we internalized these performances. The order was obviously: originally dialogue, then 'a nod and a wink', then the 'aside' said to no one in particular, then soliloquy, and finally silently thinking to oneself. Or: public prayer, individual (but still vocalized) prayer, silent prayer. Or: first reading out loud, and then reading silently to oneself. Or: doing sums with pencil and paper, doing sums by muttering and counting on one's fingers, doing it in one's head. Every mental skill and every meaningful thought that you have on tap is an internalization of something that first existed as common cultural property. It was bandied about in the public realm, and you picked it up and appropriated it for yourself.

Secondly we cannot convincingly represent thought to ourselves as consisting in anything else but a movement of words and other signs. The alternative collapses into absurdity as soon as we spell it out. Just try to imagine that you have before you two objects: one is an English sentence, and the other is a row of little latex puppets, thoughts made of mind-stuff. Now you have to decide whether the former is 'an accurate representation' of the latter. That's ridiculous. A word is not like anything else but another word. And in any case, what sort of 'putting into' is the putting of thoughts into words? The only possible answer is, saying them out loud. So thoughts are words, as yet unspoken. That's all thoughts are.

Thirdly, human societies can't function unless people think and feel alike. And in fact we see every day how members of the same society achieve a most minute and delicate mutual attunement in their vocabulary and body-language. That is how a culture is maintained, and it leaves no room for the kind of pessimistic individualism which isolates each self in solitary confinement, thinking solitary thoughts. Biological and social considerations surely make it clear that subjective consciousness was first constructed, not in order that we should learn to think and feel for ourselves, but to enable us to feel more deeply for and with others. Language cuts so deep into our souls that we can be quite sure that we are pretty much alike inside – so far as we have any 'inside', that is.

Fourthly, for human social life to work large communities of people must be culturally programmed. And what else can this very extensive programming consist in but the mother-tongue they all share? For as we learn and profoundly internalize our

41

common language, we also learn a vast amount of shared feelings, valuations and language-games.

Fifthly, the endlessly-running character of thought just is, and cannot be conceived as being anything else but, the same property of language. One sign leads to another, and so on indefinitely. Thoughts burble on just like gossip.

Sixthly, if complex thoughts are to have some propositional force as assertions or denials or whatever, they must be syntactically ordered – which means in effect that they must be language-like. We simply cannot imagine any other way in which a sequence of mental events could amount to an assertion. 'Discursive' thought simply *has* to be linguistic: how could it not be so?

Seventhly, when people describe someone as a clear thinker, what do they ever mean, and what could they ever mean, except that she is a clear speaker, or a clear writer?

And finally, Freud, Jung and others have reminded us that a good deal of what passes for thinking is automobile, free-running, libidinally-driven fantasy: dreams, daydreams and whatnot. And the symbolism in which such thinking abounds is heavily dependent upon language: to such an extent, indeed, that even where people think they are seeing an inner picture, it is in fact the word that is the clue to the meaning of the symbol; and it is words that are doing all the work even in seemingly-pictorial dreams, even in surrealist paintings, and even where the wordplay is unconscious – as it very often is.

Now comes the killer argument, which can be summarized in a single question: 'Have you ever thought, could you ever think, of the smell of coffee just by itself, and not in association with the word coffee?' The answer is No, because the smell of coffee can exist 'in our minds' only as a ghostly feeling annexed to and formed by the word coffee.

Try, in a group of people, a simple psychological experiment. Ask them to report what comes first to mind after you utter a keyword. Pause, and say 'Breakfast'. Some of those present will say that they thought visually, of white linen and tableware and the yellow-orange-brown colours of breakfast foods: orange juice, cornflakes, egg-yolks, marmalade and so on. Others will mention sounds, the clinking of cutlery and the sizzling of the frying pan. Others, again, will think of the smells of coffee and bacon, and others will think of tastes.

From this type of experiment (first carried out by Francis Galton) it is generally concluded that people have many different kinds of mental image, associated respectively with each of the senses – vision, hearing, smell, taste. We may also have tactile and kinaesthetic images, as when we recall what it felt like to climb a mountain; and there are some people who report no images, saying that they think only in words. The notion that thinking is a picture-show in an interior theatre is so strongly-held that even this last case is not allowed to count as an exception: those highly verbal types, says the empiricist philosopher H. H. Price, must be thinking 'by means of images of words'. They look at rolling script being flashed up on the mental screen.

Such comments miss the key points, and indeed Galton himself missed the key point, which is that the experiment was after all a word-association test. What else could it have been? There is no mental screen. People only miss the obvious because realist ideology has the curious effect of making language invisible. Naturally, I am ready to allow that the way in which our word-associations run may vary according to which sort of feeling, auditory, visual or whatever, is strongest in our makeup. Thus if you are a sound recordist, the auditory feelings annexed to words will influence 'the way your mind works', as people phrase it. But 'the way your mind works' is nothing but 'the way the words run'; for it is still language that structures everything. Because (why don't people see it?) only language is publicizable. Publication, by definition, equals articulation in words. The public domain consists of all that has been published. Thus the smell of coffee only gets to be real – i.e. only gets out into the inter-personal realm – by being securely and generally annexed to the *word* coffee. It is this annexation and it alone that makes the smell of coffee into something that can be called to mind, brought up in conversation, discussed and extolled. That is why in all your days you will never find the smell of coffee spontaneously coming to mind just by itself, in the pure state and without the words. It cannot, because until language has fixed and formed it, it doesn't yet exist. Until it is named it has no definite identity. It's only a transient flicker of feeling, shapeless and therefore not-rememberable. The verbal label of 'the smell of coffee' is the necessary handle for getting hold of it and making it publicly available. Without a handle you're nothing. Only *via* words can any of our percepts be publicized, and therefore only words can build a public world for us all to inhabit.

The way people talk about reference, and about words as standing for or representing things, seems to imply that they are thinking of a relation of one-to-one correspondence or isomorphism between two distinct and independently formed objects. Perhaps they fancy that words and the world make up two independent systems. But there's only *one* thing, the feeling fixed, formed and made a public reality by such a phrase as 'the smell of coffee'. And one can define the real world as the sum of all that our language makes generally accessible and discussible. 'Reality'? – feelings fixed by conventional noises, and systematized. 'Thought'? – as the woman said to Abraham Lincoln: 'How do I know that I think 'til I hear what I say?'

If you are still not fully convinced, review the efforts currently being made by wine writers to develop a clear, agreed and generally-understood vocabulary for appraising plonk – cheapish supermarket wine. Soak yourself in the subject from nose to finish, because it is an excellent example of the way in which we use language to differentiate a realm that would otherwise (let's be honest) be featureless and flat. The wine-writer's vocabulary aims simultaneously to refine our subjective discriminations, and to structure a region of the objective world. Why? – in order to justify value-scalings. The wine-writers will have succeeded in their efforts if and when we can all of us say clearly, in an agreed vocabulary, why it is that one bottle of plonk currently costs £4.75, and another bottle only £3.25. Language's job is to structure the world, to add value and so to make life, as well as wine, more interesting.

Notes

On the boundaries of the self, see Jacques Lacan's short paper of 1949, 'The mirror stage as formative of the function of the I . . . ' (reprinted in *Écrits: a Selection*, tr. Alan Sheridan, Tavistock Publications 1977). The very early self is an arena of conflicting forces: Lacan writes about the 'aggressive disintegration' of the fragmented body. Then, when it sees its own mirror image, the infant delightedly identifies itself; and Lacan speaks of its 'jubilant assumption of its own specular image'.

I want to emphasize a third stage: we may and we often do spread ourselves over and identify ourselves with what is in earshot, what is in view, what we think of, what we call our own and what we belong to. So we should break free from the tyranny of the mirror-image and learn instead to see our selves as profoundly interwoven with our environing world. The self is large, diffuse and always 'situated'.

In retrospect, it seems curious that in Western culture we have for so long, and in so many different ways, sought to establish a clear and almost unbroken frontier between the self and its environment. One was very anxious about clean and unclean, purity and pollution, and about being composed and recollected rather than being dissipated. The belief that one was holier, better and truer when drawn back into oneself like a snail into its shell has been, in various ways, typical of the Christian ascetic, the bourgeois family with its belief in privacy and soap-and-water, and the scientific observer. But if we are ever to develop a Green culture, we must learn to enjoy 'mucking in' (and note that word).

Once again, then, we find ourselves wishing to reverse the values of much traditional spirituality. Instead of keeping ourselves to ourselves and so remaining pure, 'ecstatic immanence' is a way to happiness by mucking in and becoming thoroughly dissipated. So we should. Get stuck in!

Note the word 'earshot', just used. It is formed, apparently, on the model of bowshot, and, like many similar visual idioms, implies that perception is projective rather than just receptive. We *throw out* our interpretations, projecting meaning upon the world. Things 'feel *like*', are 'seen *as*', and 'heard *as*'. Thus we interpret, and *appropriate*, all that is within the range of our senses.

From Descartes onwards – and especially through the work of Newton – the idea grew up that we see in our heads little pictures of the way things may be out there in the world. Nonsense. I don't see in my head. I see out there, in front of me. The sailor's eyes really *do* 'sweep the horizon'. So I'm abolishing the inner theatre, and I'm spreading the self out over the world. I'm saying that the bubbling, boiling movement of language in your system is all the time turning formless feeling-events into fully-formed perceptions of an objective world out there, in front of you.

8. In the beginning is the Word

We have taken language right down to the philosophical beginning of the world – which is not the popular-scientific beginning of the world some sixteen billion years ago, but the moment-by-moment E-ventuation of Becoming. It's happening now, in you. If you concentrate, you can attend to it. At the very mouth of Becoming linguistic forms dance in your brain like fishing-flies, tempting the flux of Desire out into expression and therefore into existence. That's what your conscious and personal life consists in – a dancing play of language, animated by the same flow of Desire that it is all the time calling forth into expression, and structuring and illuminating the world of your experience.

The notion that Being and Language are co-eternal, going together back to the very beginning of things, is familiar in religious thought. The Muslim says that the Qu'ran in Arabic exists eternally in the Divine Mind; the Jew says or has said that the Torah in Classical Hebrew is similarly as old as God himself; and the Christian says that the Word through which God acts and reveals himself is consubstantial and co-eternal with God the Father. In all monotheistic traditions, God is pictured as structuring his world, legislating for it and acting in it by means of language:

> By the word of the Lord the Heavens were made,
> and all their host by the breath of his mouth . . .
> For he spoke, and it came to be;
> he commanded and it stood forth.
>
> (Psalm 33. 6, 9)

In the Qu'ran – for example in Sura XVI, The Bee – the entire created order is seen as being so full of signs that it is like the 'divine visual language' in George Berkeley's philosophy. Made of and by language, the world is a sort of living text that sings of the power and providence of its Maker.

These ancient religious doctrines do not lack profundity. I am saying that they correctly represent the philosophical situation as it is at this instant, and in your head.

It's got to be verifiably going on *now*: it cannot be referred to some other world, or to some remote time past. It's got to be demonstrably and checkably true here and now and in the motion of these very signs. For in presenting you with a philosophical text I am presenting you with nothing but a string of marks, a chain of signs and a chunk of language. That is all I can give and it's all you can get. There's nothing else: I've got to deliver *within* this line of black spidery marks on paper. I can't invoke anything prior to these marks. As a Christian I know that it's a dreadful heresy to suggest that there is or can be anything prior to language. The Word is co-eternal with the very Fount of Deity itself. So nothing is prior to language. Language goes all the way down, and in attempting to present you with a self-consistent philosophical text I cannot admit anything radically prior to or independent of this chain of signs.

Once again, if there is ever to be a satisfactory and self-consistent philosophical text, it has got to establish that the three worlds – the objective material world, the world of language and the world of consciousness – are all made of just the same stuff and indeed are all merely different ways of reading the one continuous flowing process. This has to be true, if there is to be a philosophical text that satisfactorily represents within its own movement the way that things are. If its metaphors resonate widely enough, this one strand, in the reading, may function as an epitome of the whole.

Thus the furthest and seemingly-most-paradoxical conclusions that I am trying to reach in this text are in the end best proved by being shown to be presuppositions of the very possibility of *any* satisfactory philosophical text. In the movement of words we come to feel and understand that moving energies, formed into words, are what everything's made of – and that is self-consistent, right! Our text comes full circle, democratically cancelling itself out and disclaiming any pretension to teach any novel or esoteric truth. It has done no more than show you where you are, what you are and how things are already. It has shown this by showing you that this is how things must be if there is ever to be a subject called philosophy; but, and ironically, having shown this it has thereby also shown that philosophy is an uninformative subject. It doesn't tell us any new and great Truth. All it does is help us to become happy with things as they are. It is therapy: feeling better now?

47

Hugh Rayment-Pickard interestingly points out 'a direct etymological link between therapy and homeliness. My Greek dictionary has *therapeia* meaning a remedy, but also a household servant. *Therapõn* means someone with responsibility for looking after the household of an important person. *Therapein* are household gods or idols ... the therapist is the person who makes you feel at home, who brings the gods (Hebrew, *Teraphim*) into your house and attends on you.'

Compare this with the argument in the Appendix on Kingdom-theology, below. In the past we ejected the gods from our home, and projected them out into a separate, sacred world. Then, with the help of the doctrine of metaphysical evil and the soul-body distinction, we taught ourselves to feel that we are aliens in this world, who must look to the Sacred World above to find our true home. But I am arguing that we should now be reversing all that, and returning the gods into our hearts, our homes, *this* world.

9. What matter?

We have found that all our thinking is transacted in signs, which is to say that it involves a bubbling, outpouring motion of language. Many twentieth-century writers have attempted to represent the stream of consciousness, and inevitably – rightly – they have portrayed it as a rambling and disorderly, but by no means pointless, stream of words. Like Molly Bloom's soliloquy at the end of *Ulysses*. And this babbling to oneself goes on also in the Unconscious. We should free ourselves from the notion that the Unconscious is 'the beast beneath the skin', a system of rapacious biological drives. The Unconscious is already cultural, for it trades in symbols. Above all – as every comedian knows –it loves word-play and *double entendre*. It may be highly active in words at just those moments when, at the conscious level, we think we are quite speechless.

So language goes all the way down to the limit of thought, at the point where Becoming emerges into the light of significance. (No: it emerges precisely as it is lit up with significance.) And it follows that we ourselves live always inside language. We are not up against objective reality directly, as some people seem to be trying to say: we are always inside our cultural sign-system. (As we are now, while I write and you read; and a good thing too, for if we were not always within our present situation this text would have no chance of telling all the truth.)

Yesterday, on a winter's afternoon, I stood in Ely Cathedral looking at the biblical scenes and figures of saints in its stained-glass windows. All this iconography and all these pictures are part of the Cathedral's own *internal* sign-system. They are lit up from outside by the declining sun, but one cannot see through the glass. An epistemological realist is like a person who assumes that the windows are transparent, and that through them we see coloured figures standing outside the building. That is a mistaken view of the situation. All one sees is that certain signs – components of a coherent system that functions *within* the building – have become lit up. At least in the main body of the Cathedral, there is no clear glass at all, and yesterday was a very dull afternoon. The windows were evidently being illuminated, but there was no direct way of telling how or by what.

That a Cathedral is an image of the human body has often been said. It is also a very complex and highly-organized sign-system. So Ely Cathedral may be taken as illustrating the way in which all our thinking, *and therefore our whole life*, is lived inside the cultural sign-system that gives us our form of consciousness and prescribes our world-view. As for perception, the analogy suggests that, since there is no clear glass, we can know only that it involves the illumination or activation of signs. Suppose that the entire sensory surface of the human body, including the eardrums, the retinas, the nasal membranes, the skin and so forth, has got words over it, just as all the glazing of Ely Cathedral is filled with stained-glass images. Then, much as sunlight illuminates the figures in the Ely glass, so it is as if external events impinging upon my sensitive surfaces activate words.

Pressing the analogy further, suppose that I have never left the Cathedral, just as I have never lived outside the language written on my body: then in both cases I'll have to limit myself to saying that the signs became lit up – as if from outside, maybe, but I'm pretty unsure about the inside-outside distinction. Without ever having been 'outside', how can I make it?

49

I'm using the analogy to introduce a theory of knowledge somewhere between naive realism and the most thoroughgoing constructivism. The one sees the eye as a camera; the other sees it as a cine-projector. To the naive realist the human eye is like a camera, an instrument which proverbially 'cannot lie'. The eye reflects what it sees like a mirror: we see an independent world just as it is. By contrast, the thoroughgoing constructivist sees the human eye as more like a cine-projector. Your visual field is the screen, and your life-energy or libido provides the power-source. You project out upon the Void a world of your own creation, a world that reflects your beliefs, your desires, your fantasies, and above all, your language.

If that is so, why does the world we project out look the way it does? There are two chief sets of constraints, one biological and the other socio-cultural. The biological constraints prescribe that we must construct a world that we can inhabit, a world by which we can orient ourselves, maintain our lives and fulfil our desires. More than that, it has to be a 'sexy' world, in the broad sense of being a world that excites rather than quenches our own zest for life. That is why the world we see is a world already painted over and charged up with our human feelings. And, secondly, there are the social constraints: these prescribe that if we are to have a common language (as we must), then we must with others build a common or public world, a world of social interaction, social training, and continual communication. In fact they prescribe that the social world has to take the form of a very large playing-field upon which a great number of overlapping games are being played. People are moving about with, for the most part, remarkable ease, joining and participating now in one game, now in another.

Earlier, we reduced thought to a motion of language, and perception to the activation of cultural signs on the surface of the body. Now we link the whole cultural sign-system with the conception of the social world as a sports hall in which many different games are being played. Signs as insignia. Notice that the entire cultural sign-system that we inhabit is produced, lives, moves and slowly evolves in and through the playing of the various games.

From this last point it follows that radical constructivism

cannot possibly lead to general nihilism, or reduce all reality to a dream. If the apparent world around us has to be regarded as a projection, somebody or some community is doing the projecting, and doing it in some interest or for some reason. Time is passing, energy is being expended.

So let us ask what there must be, even on the most thoroughgoing constructivist account.

There must at least be language; for language is something, one of the very, very few things, whose existence cannot self-consistently be denied, denial being in itself a linguistic act. And language is now moving, for this sentence is being read. So the world is at least a communications network, with messages of many kinds flying around, along (no doubt) various channels. The motion of language takes time, so there is temporality, and it always requires a material vehicle that it forms and rides upon. We see this vehicle as a discharge of energies. And from what is said by the users of language, we learn that the flowing discharge of energies in which their living consists is formed by language into a complex, highly-differentiated life of consciously-felt feelings.

The vocabulary in which human subjectivity is constructed includes all the words linked with sensory qualities such as colour, taste, smell and so forth, and all the words in which speakers voice their emotions, desires, beliefs, intentions and so forth. In discussing 'the smell of coffee' we have already shown the marvellous way in which the phrase fixes, forms, makes repeatedly accessible and therefore objective, makes conscious and makes valuable what would otherwise be a mere transient and instantly-lost episode in the flux of our life-energies. Our feelings are able to *live* as constituent parts of a public world when they are firmly annexed to the words that give us a handle on them. And that a word is a 'handle' is just the sort of elegant philosophical point that is much more tellingly made when we hear it in cockney than when we hear it in Balliol.

Language, then, turns the physical process of our life into voiced feelings bonded to words, and the peculiarly powerful association between words and feelings makes poetry possible. But there is no mind in the old, strong sense. There is no need to postulate a separate, isolated inner world of consciousness, made of mind-stuff and washed over by waves of emotion, in which something called reason carries out mental operations as it processes the beliefs, memories and other materials it has in store. All that (read realistically, I mean) is what we described as a construction. It's a cultural fiction, and one we will be happier without. We do better to equate the world of consciousness with the *public* world before us. The field of consciousness is the field of view, the life-world.

The 'mind', then, does not really exist. But there is a rich language-formed discharge of energies. Your body is itself a system of energies covered all over with language, in such a way that as things and people bump into you in the rough and tumble of life, it clicks and whirrs, flickers and flashes just like a pin-ball machine in an amusement arcade. All that pinging and flashing on your body-surface is real enough, and the sensations of pleasure that accompany the goings-on are real enough too (the smell and taste of coffee being a case in point). But the elaborate constructed world of subjective consciousness, no: that is no more than a rather flickery, strobey picture conjured up by the language-events occurring upon your surface. 'The mind' is not a queer kind of inner space *behind* our faces, but an interpretation of the way the signs are moving *in front of* our faces, out there in the common world.

The non-realist view of the mind sees it not as a thing, but as an interpretation. (You object? Listen: if I challenge you to show me a mind, all you'll ever be able to show me is what I have defined the mind as being. We read people's minds by reading their language and their body-language, don't we? So 'the mind' is the meaning of the body-language, and you'd better admit that I'm right.) But what about the common world? Because the linguistic sign is unstable and only conventional, for there to be living language there must be social interaction. Language is maintained in working order by all the ways in which you and I negotiate our daily encounters and 'keep going'. So, all that there *has* to be of an objective world – and indeed all that most people notice, for most of the time – is the social world, the communications network, the world of drama.

Here we pause for a moment to consider the objection of commonsense. Surely if we know anything we know that in modern times there has been a huge development of objective empirical knowledge of a real physical world around us? What about, for example, the physical and biological sciences?

Suppose we are setting off for a country walk. Well prepared, we take with us a 1:25000 map, a guide-book, a flora and a bird-book. These works are so beautiful nowadays, and produced to such an astonishingly high standard, that we can be quite sure that they give us minutely detailed and accurate information about what we will meet in the region in which we are walking.

Yes, yes: but the maps and guides don't present us with the world itself, but with the world that is encoded into our human sign-systems. Coupled with our earlier realization that all our thinking is transacted in language, this reminds us that even out in the open country we are still just as much within the world of human signs as we would be if we were in the Wanchai district of Hong Kong at 11 p.m. We always see a world that is already covered all over with human language, with our human feeling-responses plastered over it, and interpreted by human theories. Even just looking up into the empty blue sky, I no longer see the solid glassy blue firmament that our remoter ancestors saw; I see empty space. I see 'the sky', 'blue', cool and blissful – and those epithets remind me that even when I am looking up into the empty blue sky I am looking into the endless symbolic life of humanity.

What I see here is, metaphysically speaking, the same as what we found when we lay reflecting introspectively and quietly in bed at dead of night; the same as we found when considering the nature of thought and language; and the same as we found when we were standing in Ely Cathedral looking up at the stained glass. That is to say, because the self and language and the world are all made of the same continuous flowing stuff, you'll come in the end to the same result, wherever you start from. What presents itself is like a fountain. It is the flux of Becoming, a ceaseless, still, self-renewing Now, an outpouring and scattering of featherlight dancing energies-read-as-signs. It conjoins word and flesh, meanings and feelings, poetry and physics. And in so far as it implies a kind of cosmic humanism, it is a very widespread theme in world religions. It is Anthropos, it is the Macrocosm, it is the Dharma-body of the Buddha, it is the cosmic Christ. It is holy ground: it is everydayness. It is an idea that we can reach if and when we can in philosophy overcome the old dualism between mind and body, the inner world and the outer world, and so come to see our own lives as continuous with the eternally-transient, endlessly self-renewing, cosmic-yet-also-human symbolic life of the Whole.

10. The eye and the ear

The dominant tradition in Western thought as founded by Plato has always based its metaphysical assumptions and its metaphors upon the supposed priority of the eye and the sense of sight. This priority is assumed so deeply and is so pervasive that it is hard to take the full measure of it. To quote just two familiar examples from the language of religion: almost anyone may hear God, in this life. No special faculties are needed. But *seeing* God – that's different: that's getting really close, so close that it must be strictly reserved for the Blessed and the world to come. Seeing, indeed, is so special, and so far superior to every other sense, that merely to have seen the consecrated Host at the Mass was enough. Despite Christ's own words of institution, you did not need actually to taste the Bread of Heaven: it was enough to feast your eyes.

Thinkers have noticed the oddity of all this from time to time. Nietzsche complains about the great unblinking Cyclopean eye of Socrates. The botanist Agnes Arber wrote a good book, *The Mind and the Eye* (Cambridge 1954), about the extent to which most of us, but perhaps especially 'trained observers' (i.e., scientists) tend to equate the eye with the I. We like to fancy, don't we, that the eye is the most expressive part of the face, and that it is not only a window for the soul to look out of but also a window into the soul? In a half-witted mood, I peer into my lady's eye and see there a tiny image of myself – evidence, I hope, that I am foremost in her thoughts; and evidence too for the origin of the notion that thoughts are little visual images in the mind, just like the little images to be seen in the fund of an eye.

(Come to think of it, though, these considerations are perhaps not so very gratifying. For just how large do I bulk in my lady's eyes? Peering again, I estimate, about 2mm. At most.)

Michel Foucault, writing about the Enlightenment, has reminded us of the way the eye wants things to keep still so that it can see them clearly and get a good eyeful. The eye has, indeed, no special liking for time and movement. A twitchy herbivorous past, perhaps, has left us uneasy about sudden movements. The eye's preference is for a diagrammatized world with everything spread out in space, pinned down, tabulated – laid out on a surface, a *tabula*, like goods in a shop-window – classified, arranged, ordered like a wall chart, like the periodic table of the elements, like a family tree or the London Underground map.

What metaphors do we use to express a full and satisfactory understanding of a matter? Naturally, optical metaphors – metaphors of lucidity, transparency and clear, unclouded vision. The eye demands bright illumination, freedom from obscurity or ambiguity, leisurely contemplation of a motionless object, and a metaphysics of substance that describes a world made of distinct things with qualities. Inevitably, the mind is seen as a mirror of the world, or alternatively a theatre in which thoughts move like little images. We picture an imagined course of events as an interior picture-show that the inward eye simultaneously directs and observes, rather as Victorian children used to entertain themselves by staging plays with cut-out paper characters that they moved about in toy theatres.

It is very hard to get away from images and metaphors which have become so deeply embedded in the language. People are to a quite extraordinary degree convinced that when they are imagining things they have a picture-show going on in their heads. but the very strength of their conviction only goes to show the astounding power of language to create 'feels', secondary qualities, imaginary entities, spaces, worlds.

For there is no such picture show. Yes, I do allow that there are tides and surges of formless, inchoate endogenous feeling. And there are (as we have so often argued) the very powerful and vivid feelings annexed to words, evoked by them and spread by and with them over the constructed life-world of sense-experience. There is a theatre-show *out there* all right; but remember, on the doctrine I am urging the traditional inner world of the mind and the traditional objective world are best seen as effectively coinciding. The true 'mental' field or theatre is best regarded as that which we are presently looking at, listening to, doing, saying. It is what we are concerned with, what 'fills our thoughts'; and as for the fancied inner world, it is by comparison something very, very faint, no more than a phantasm, a ghost-world conjured up by the motion of not-fully-articulated language in our physical systems. It is like a simulation. Your *real* feeling-life is elsewhere; it is spread over what is out there in front of your nose.

This is all very difficult, but do you see the shift I am trying to bring about? I want to undermine the vision-based interior/exterior contrast. The received metaphors set up a contrast between two spaces and two worlds, one inside and one outside. Through the outward, carnal eye we look out into the objective space of the external world much as a woman might look out of the window of her house to see what is going on. But when she feels *reflective* she draws close the curtains, turns about and perhaps switches on a light so that she can look around indoors. Introspection, looking within.

Just as there is an inward eye that looks back into the interior space of the mind, so our metaphors suggest also that there is an inner light. Consciousness, reflection, is a well-lit drawing room, whereas the Unconscious is a dimly-lit region below stairs, like the kitchen or boiler-room. Processes going on there help to sustain drawing-room life, no doubt, but it's not a region that drawing-room folk care to enquire into too closely. And is it not curious that the analogy between a house and the human body is so very close?

Now, it is a consequence of the whole argument being pressed here that we need to escape from some at least of the effects of the historic dominance of the eye and the metaphors of vision. We will do better instead to think in terms of the (logical) priority of the ear and language. The ear is a better philosopher, I suggest for three very obvious reasons. The first is that the ear cannot so easily as the eye pretend that its experience is or might be extra-temporal. We may dream of a timeless contemplative vision, but we can hardly suppose that there could be timeless hearing of anything.

Secondly, because hearing is relatively more inward anyway, it does not seem to give rise to, or feel so much need for, any sharp inner/outer distinction. Indeed, it is most difficult to make any such distinction, as sufferers from tinnitus and 'humming' know. We speak of an 'inward eye' which looks at visual images and memories, but we simply do not have corresponding phrases relating to hearing. There is no 'minds's ear', or 'inward ear'.

Thirdly, the ear and the word are more closely related to moral action and the shaping of life than are the eye and things seen. This shows very well in the use of 'word', 'words', to mean various sorts of stimulus to action. Having a few words with someone, we are prompting them, reminding them, reproaching them, requesting them, warning them, encouraging them and so on. There is still some truth in the old cliché that Greek culture, being based on the primacy of the eye, was more oriented towards theory, the visual arts and a contemplative spirituality; whereas Jewish culture, being based on the primacy of the word and hearing, was more oriented towards music, verbal dialectics, conduct and an ethical spirituality.

At this point Derrida says that 'We live in the difference between the Jew and the Greek', and goes on to end his essay by quoting Joyce: 'Jewgreek is greekjew. Extremes meet' ('Violence and Metaphysics'; in *Writing and Difference*, ET Routledge 1978, p. 153). Very well, but the point that I have been making – or belabouring – is still worth insisting upon. The language remains full of the old visual metaphors, a scientific education still has the effect of entrenching them yet more firmly, and (one might say) our commonsense is still too Cartesian, even today.

The more visual one is, the harder the correction is to make. I have tried to force the issue by using seemingly counter-intuitive arguments to the effect that the perceived qualities and tones of the world of experience are all language-linked and language-formed. We don't first perceive qualities and tones such as colours, sounds, tastes and smells, and only *then* try to find words for them. Rather, it's the other way round. Experience only comes out into the light of consciousness in so far as it has been evoked by language, coloured by language, and further enriched and elaborated by the associations between words, and therefore also between their respective annexed feeling-tones.

57

So in trying to move my thinking and yours from the metaphysics of the eye towards a metaphysics of the ear I am trying to get closer to what I take to be the actual metaphysical situation.

There is a striking corollary, which has already been mentioned. The objective world suddenly gets to look a good deal more humanoid than we had thought possible. From Blaise Pascal to Max Weber the sages have lamented the 'disenchantment' of the scientific world-picture. But now the world begins to look like the Macrocosm once more. It *speaks* to us – mostly in prose, but sometimes pure poetry.

11. Cosmic humanism

During the twentieth century it has been common – at least on the part of Arts-educated people with a certain mistrust of science – to suggest that the human being is now alienated and homeless in a disenchanted Universe. Heidegger, rather shockingly but very influentially, sees objects in the world around us as mere stuff at hand, to be picked up and made use of as need arises. When we thus see the world as a scrapyard, it is not surprising that we come to see ourselves too as bits of scrap: we are where we have been casually thrown, lost, out-of-place, homeless, driftwood. In Iris Murdoch's *Nuns and Soldiers* (1980) Christ himself becomes a casual young cosmic drifter who warns Anne, almost in the tones of Nietzsche and Sartre, that she's on her own now. The poet A. E. Housman says what this feels like: he is 'alone and afraid/in a world I never made'.

The feeling that our new cosmology is chilly and inhuman must surely reflect a lack of knowledge of science – indeed, a fear and suspicion of science – which has been too common amongst writers. Fortunately the history of painting teaches rather the opposite lesson: from Brunelleschi onwards the painter's eye profits immensely from the study of geometrical optics, and from Vesalius and others onwards it is generally acknowledged that by studying their anatomy one greatly enriches one's perception of animal and human bodies. More recently, an irregular line of

58

painters have profited by studying colour science and the psychology of vision.

This notion, that scientific theory may actually enhance one's perception of the world and make the world more beautiful, now needs to be pressed much harder. For today when you look at the night sky, when you look at landscape, when you look at plant and animal bodies, and even when you look at materials such as wood and stone, you are looking at something that we made. It has long been easy to read the history of a church, or of a whole town, by walking around it, and nowadays it is equally easy to read the geological and economic history of a landscape as one walks over it. It is also easy for a biology-trained person to read its evolutionary history and its way of life off the body of a plant or an animal. Looking at the sun, the moon and the night sky, our perception of them is formed and enriched by the great complexity of modern physical and cosmological theory. Science has educated our senses.

Everywhere now we see a world enriched by our own knowledge-systems, our own *logos*, our own theory. We made the world we see – and the application of that assertion is much wider and more radical than I have yet indicated, because all the qualities of perceptual experience from which science starts – all the looks, noises, tastes, smells and feels – are themselves *also* human products. Perceptual qualities, as we have argued earlier, are feelings produced by and annexed to words. That is why, for example, in post-structuralist philosophy, in religious thought, and in Berkeley's 'Divine visual language', it comes to be recognized that our entire world is made of signs. *Human* signs, feeling-responses, symbols, reminders, connections.

Look at your own perceptual experience. Look at your visual field. Carry out a Kant-type transcendental analysis of what's in front of you. Ask how it is that you see things, identifiable things, describable things with qualities, disposed in space and persisting in time. You will find that everything that is given to you is already human: human the general conceptual framework in which all things are set; human all the categories through which they are thought; human the scientific theory through which everything can be identified, understood and described; human the feeling-responses that we call the perceptual qualities, such as colour and taste; and human all the language in which alone you and I can say, think and check out all this. Our world is now a human world all the way down. We have gradually evolved amongst ourselves every bit of what we see. Our world is our own accumulated *oeuvre*, our self-objectification.

Once people believed themselves to be at home in the Universe in a much more modest sense. As they saw it, our human reason was a participation in cosmic Reason, and the human mind was made in the image of God. There was a pre-established reciprocal adaptation between thought and being, so that the world was seen as having been created to be a fitting stage for human life. The world was like a house, with built-in rules that we could quite easily find out and follow.

Early modern science did for a while, and in some minds at least, appear to overthrow this picture. But my argument is that nowadays the world has again become our world, and in a much stronger sense than before. If we are microcosm then the world is now Macrocosm. It is the Scandinavian Ymir, the Indian Purusha, the Chinese P'an-ku; it is Anthropos, the concrete universal human over against us, which we have generated, out of which we have come, into which we will return. And it is beautiful.

To radicalize humanism into pantheism may seem a bold move, but there are many precedents. In Buddhism, for example, the word *dharma* has a wide range of uses extending from 'elementary constituent of the world' to 'element of the Buddha's teaching'. Here again we meet the idea that the world is made of signs, and experience is to be read – an idea that is wittily illustrated by the Japanese brushwork that sometimes deliberately makes calligraphy and botanical illustration indistinguishable from each other. But further: in Buddhism, the self itself is merely a collection of the constituents of the world. From this naturalistic reduction of the self it follows that any bit of the world may turn out to be a bit of a person, or a bit of a communication. Indeed, as I've argued elsewhere, it may turn out to be a bit of more than one person at once. From one angle it may be read as a bit of me, and from another angle it may be read as a bit of the Buddha, or of Christ. Anything, everything may particpate in Buddhahood, or Buddha-nature: anything, everything may be read as part of the cosmic Body of Christ.

Lest it seem that we are leaving the domain of philosophy, I should emphasize here that if we speak of the world over against ourselves as a sort of super-person, we simply use a metaphor. It cannot be more than that: but it is a permissible and an interesting metaphor, whose use in religion is compatible with our generally naturalistic outlook. In the West (although we have had our Spinoza) there are still people who are nervous about a philosophical policy of thoroughgoing naturalism and reduction; but Buddhism shows that such a policy can have the unexpected consequence of giving a clear meaning, for the first time, to some old religious idioms. That can't be all bad.

A further twist in the argument now follows. Cosmic humanism is, no doubt, a two-way, reciprocal reduction by which our humanity becomes a mere transient product of nature and nature an expressive product of our humanity. The middle term into which, from opposite sides, everything is brought down is the flux of language-events. Fine. But (some will object) isn't this humanization of everything diminishing and narcissistic? Isn't it rather disgusting to compose a metaphysics that pictures us humans as caught up forever in an outsideless dream of ourselves from which there can be no awakening?

We need to be cured of the unworthy gut-reaction here. Is it any objection to Rothko's paintings or to Nietzsche's philosophy that in each case the oeuvre is only the personal expression of a man who was a pretty poor and sad creature? Are human natural languages, in all their subtlety and complexity, diminished when it is pointed out that they are merely the outcome of many unplanned and casual human goings-on?

Our argument as a whole will show, as I hope, that a cosmic religious humanism need not be thought of as in any way spiritually diminishing. Rather the opposite.

Notes

My cosmic humanism is not as new as it may seem. In antiquity religious thought was uninhibitedly anthropomorphic, and people saw gods – human-shaped gods – everywhere in the natural world around them. There were gods of the Sun and Moon, of the sky and the winds, of Earth and ocean, of mountains and rivers. Everything was 'full of gods', as

Thales reportedly said; and what is striking in this is the way people saw in the cosmos around them evidence of a *humanlike* integrity and perfection that they felt was lacking in themselves. They looked outwards: they looked to the world of the gods, which was also the cosmos, for redemption, and desired union with it in death. Thus in Egyptian tombs the dead person is surrounded by painted images of the earth and the sky.

So the cosmic religious humanism here put forward has something in common with the 'cosmic religion' of antiquity. It becomes attractive again as an option when one feels dissatisfied with the other possibilities – chiefly those offered by Hegel and Kierkegaard. In the end for Hegel one *becomes* God, achieving total lucidity and autonomy. That is subjective redemption, and few of us desire it now. Reacting against Hegel, Kierkegaard reaffirms the Otherness of God. Faith in its anguish confronts a God who is an infinite Wall of black marble – and I fear that at the end of his life Kierkegaard was destroyed by his own faith.

My 'expressionist' cosmic humanism offers a way to an objective redemption. We are drawn out of ourselves, we want to die *into* the sunset and the sea, because it was we who evolved this dazzling beauty. It's human; we taught ourselves to see all of Nature as Buddha-nature, and the cosmos as the Body of Christ. We slowly evolved amongst ourselves what turns out to be our chief final consolation.

A passing tribute should be paid here to the French photographer Robert Doisneau, who coined the phrase 'the religion of looking', and who died as this book was being written.

Commenting, a friend asks whether I am arguing for a stronger or a weaker version of humanism. On the strong interpretation, I am seeking to escape from the vertigo of Hegel's bad infinity (a world endlessly transient and unstable in all directions) by making the human self into a new Sacred Centre that organizes everything in relation to itself.

But that is not what I am saying. The present argument tries to bring about a feeling of liberation by performing *a double reduction*. Both the objective world on the far side, and subjective selfhood on the near side, are brought down into the stream of always-already-language-formed events. When the double reduction is carried through, we realize that all things are ours, because everything is in principle intelligible, and nothing is intractably alien or hostile to us. That is the 'ecstatic immanence' which we enjoy when we are completely given to, identified with and lost in the flux of our own life. It calls for a kind of outgoing self-abandonment, my 'expressionism'. Weak humanism, if you will.

Cosmic humanism is not only a mythological theme: it is also a philosophical commonplace. In metaphysical systems there is very commonly an analogy between the self and the cosmos. Thus, for example, the soul-body distinction may parallel the God-world distinction; and see the comment about Schopenhauer in the *Prosopography*. Spinoza and Kant are further examples of philosophers whose anthropology mirrors their cosmology: and quite right too, say I.

12. The fountain

I am arguing for a philosophical outlook that is monistic and naturalistic. It is monistic in the sense that everything, including the objective world, language, and the world of subjectivity is made of only one sort of stuff; and it is naturalistic in the sense that everything is contingent. Nothing is entrenched, necessary or absolute; everything is relative and fleeting. It just happens to have come to be the way it is, and in due course it will pass away.

We ask, then, what is this one sort of stuff of which everything is made? And we have answered that there is at least language in motion; and therefore there is also at least a discharge and scattering of energies, and there is temporality. There are also organisms like us, temporarily self-maintaining systems of energies which keep themselves going by extracting energy from their immediate environment. These organisms are in a slightly prickly and ambivalent relationship to each other, for they compete for the available resources, but must also co-operate in order to survive and reproduce. In order to resolve this ambivalence they ritualize their relations and develop forms of symbolic exchange. Thus language enters, and in due course completes the world, by making it possible for a bit of the world-process – and even *this* bit, your reading of this paragraph now – to be a symbolic representation of the whole.

That paragraph gives the difference between physics and metaphysics. Nobody can or should deny the great power and beauty of modern physics, and the distinction of its leading practitioners. But physical cosmology of the sort practised today leaves out of the story it tells something essential, namely an account of how it is that within the cosmos thus represented there has emerged the possibility of representing it. That is, a good cosmology has to be reflexively self-consistent. It won't make me truly happy unless, while it is explaining the cosmos, it is simultaneously looping back and explaining itself, accounting for its own possibility. Thus our philosophical happiness requires, not just a physical cosmology, but a metaphysical cosmology which shows us, and enables us without any remainder to understand and accept, our unity with the whole.

Can we imagine that the objective world similarly loops back and explains itself? Yes, but only in a parable (something 'thrown out') because *ex hypothesi* nobody could ever occupy the standpoint for verifying the story we are about to tell. The parable, we will see, has something badly wrong with it; but there is nevertheless also something to be learned from it.

Imagine the universe as a torus, a great fat doughnut-shape with a very small central hole. Sliced horizontally, flat along the line of its outer circumference, it is one circle; sliced vertically across the middle, like a cake cut in half, it will present two circles just touching at a point.

That point of contact is the so-called 'initial singularity' of physical cosmology, from which the Big Bang begins. From it a stream of energies flows upwards and arcs out over the whole surface of the torus, curving down again as it spreads until at the outer circumference of the torus the moment of the universe's greatest expansion is reached. It doesn't stop, but flows on as the contraction phase begins. Now the tide turns inwards under and back into the central black hole again, bringing the entire process full circle.

Now imagine that the whole process is self-sustaining, as with a fountain that continuously recycles its own water. The end of the process circles back to become its beginning again. But because the whole process is continuous, the universe is always at every stage of its own endless life.

The eternal return happens in effect only once, because it is always the return of exactly the same. The ideal observer sees a streaming stillness in which everything is unchangingly transient. In fact, the torus looks like the Rose at the end of Dante's *Paradiso*. All the equations balance out, so that the energy accumulated during the contraction phase precisely equals the energy released during the expansion phase. The initial explosion and the final black hole coincide, and in any case neither is in any way special. The torus has neither a first Beginning nor a last End. It has no outside, and calls for no further explanation. Its life is one continuous and timeless cycle.

So on this model, or parable, the universe is an outsideless, beginningless, endless and foundationless whole, a flux of pure contingency that slips away at the speed of light – so fast that it eternally brings itself back again. It thus renews itself eternally, like Shiva's fire. As for you and me, we are motes moving somewhere on the upper face of the torus. Time has an arrow, a direction for us of course; but the process as a whole has no history. It's not going anywhere – but then, *we* aren't going anywhere, either. We are going everywhere, out into the flow.

Next, of course, take away (if you were imagining it) the solid geometrical form of the torus, and see it as consisting of nothing else but the streaming flux and reflux of the energies of which it is composed. Yes, it is like a fountain that perpetually renews itself by recycling its own waters; and a fountain is a traditional symbol of life and healing, refreshment and repose. As Asian thought would put it, the universe is Empty – i.e., there is no enduring substance – but in that very Emptiness is found the bliss of Nirvana. And to make a similar point in Western terms, every bit of the fountain, every scattering droplet, is so utterly ephemeral that the entire fountain seems motionless in its ceaseless activity, like the God of Aristotle.

That is the trickiest bit of the argument for a Western mind to grasp. The claim is that the more we can come to view everything, including ourselves, as nothing but a self-perpetuating flux of transient phenomena, the happier and more liberated we will become. Eternity and transience, nothingness and bliss coincide.

Why are we puzzled by this? We are puzzled because such a long tradition in the West has taught us to assume that the relative must follow and proceed from an absolute Ground, that things temporal must be viewed as proceeding forth from the eternal order, that the contingent must be grounded in the necessary and so on. We are intensely habituated and committed to these ways of thinking, and at first sight don't see how we could do without them. Thus, when I say that the world presents itself as a dense stream of language-formed events, you immediately start to wonder where Becoming 'comes from' – and that long Western tradition has you assuming that the realm of Becoming has just obviously *got* to be viewed as proceeding from and grounded in a realm of eternal Being.

I question this for two main reasons. First, because none of us can even begin to imagine or describe exactly *how* the contingent and fleeting issues forth from the necessary and eternal. The old metaphysical contrasts and foundationalist ways of thinking, derived from Greek metaphysics, were so entrenched in the language that we did not stop to question them. It just seemed obvious that the changing world needed to have an unchanging Ground. But why? And exactly *how* are we to think of the changing as coming forth from the unchanging? As soon as the questions are posed, we begin to suspect that much of Western philosophy was just as tradition-dependent as Western theology. It *seemed* intelligible – but for no better reason than that it was habitual. And in the second place, the torus parable and the fountain metaphor do suggest to me at least that, despite the very long tradition that says otherwise, we might nevertheless one day learn to find peace of soul and eternal happiness in contemplating pure speed-of-light transience.

In fact, very often we use symbols of transience as aids to meditation: a flower, a light breeze moving through leaves, sunlight on water, waves breaking on a beach.

So the torus-parable may do a job in helping to free our minds from various traditional, and now objectionable, philosophical assumptions. An old, old tradition still tries to persuade us that all this, the passing show of life, can't exist just on its own. But perhaps it can? Perhaps the flux of things does not need to be supported by any independent ground; perhaps the quest for substance – solid, enduring independent being – is neurotic, and our highest happiness is to dance away out into the flux; perhaps the world does not, like a story, need to have a beginning, a middle and an end; and perhaps it doesn't have to be the case that each event and each deed is in the old sense 'once and for all', eternally decisive.

All that said however, it must again be emphasized that there is something wrong with the torus-parable. In the terms proposed earlier, it is physics and not metaphysics: it is a thought-experiment and a cosmological hypothesis, but it does not include anything to explain its own possibility. On the contrary, it proposes an impossibility, by being written from a narrative standpoint outside the outsideless – i.e., from a viewpoint that cannot exist. In addition, it fails to make any connection between the moving energies *of* which it speaks, and the chain of signs *in* which it speaks.

So the torus image was only a corrective fiction, a story told in order to help us free ourselves from certain outdated assumptions. As for its limitations, they recall us to the primacy of the ordinary-life-world. We constructed the ordinary-life-world from the standpoint of our human experience. It presents itself as a stream of events that are language-formed all the way down. As soon as the world of Becoming comes forth, it is already formed, lit up by language. The smell of coffee, for example, as soon as we feel it, is already tied to and recognized through the *phrase* 'the smell of coffee'. The words single out a scrap of felt experience, form it, make something of it, identify it and give us a handle on it. So there is a life of conscious feeling, and it is all stuck to language. Each day a vast number of linguistic and other signs pass through us. Some we send, others we receive, and others again are spontaneously-generated within our systems. These signs have feelings of many kinds annexed to them, and their flowing, joined up, is our life of feeling. But the life of feeling does not exist independently of or prior to the language that pro-duces it, brings it forth.

So on the account I am trying to give, it is in the ordinary-life-world that everything hangs together, and everything makes sense. The flow of language-formed events produces on its outer face the process of social life in the everyday world, and on its inner face the life of subjective feeling.

Note

A friend, Bernard Brown, charges me with being 'a Rilke-Epigone', and points out that Rainer Maria Rilke was fascinated by the fountain-image. The best-known example is *Römische Fontäne*, but there is also a late poem in French, *La fontaine*, in which the fountain symbolizes the eternal return.

The old – i.e., Renaissance – idea that poetic utterance, *Dichtung*, can form and beautify the world and redeem our life may have passed from Rilke to Heidegger. See the latter's *Poetry, Language, Thought*, tr. Hofstadter, New York: Harper 1971, 1975. In these late pieces, Heidegger has moved a long way from the dismal utilitarianism of his early view of things-in-the-world (*innerweltliches Seiendes*), mentioned earlier.

I should draw attention to the fact that the torus-parable as here presented changes a little the doctrine put forward in *After All* (p. 78). There, I said that 'the scientific story that we now tell has been developed as a sort of possibility-condition. Present-day ways of describing the world, when analysed, require us to tell such-and-such a story about the past. Our capacity to verbalize and so finish the world thus, as it were, circles back to the beginning and makes the Big Bang and cosmic evolution real in retrospect.' *Ex hypothesi*, nobody could have de-scribed-and-observed such events as they happened; and they 'have had to wait for a strange retroactive realization, given to them by us in modern scientific theory'.

Here, I have modified that doctrine slightly. The torus-image invokes the traditional image of eternity as a circle. Everything is transient and everything flits away at the speed of light, thereby also bringing itself back again, so that the Universe is eternally at all stages of its own life-cycle. You might think that we could then go on to argue that, if the Universe is formed, illuminated and made real by our representation of it at any *one* moment in its eternal return, then it is thereby formed, illuminated and made real at *all* moments.

This would happen by a version of the old cosmological argument. That argument claims that, for all the later stages to be real, the First Cause has to be real. The adapted version of the argument will claim that, if the cosmos becomes real in our present theory of it, then all the earlier stages in cosmic history, through which it eternally comes to be what it is now, must also be real. So, in this adapted version of the Cosmological Argument, the present moment, in which we describe and theorize the world, will take the place of the First Cause. It will be the present moment that makes everything else real.

Such an argument, however, would reintroduce metaphysics in too strong a sense, and is incompatible with this book's emphasis on the priority of biology and ordinariness. Indeed, at the present time there is a danger that the public will attach too much religious significance to the rather fanciful cosmological speculations of a few physicists, and disagreeable personality-cults may develop. Nor do I wish to side with the mad astronomer in Dr Johnson's *Rasselas*, who came to think that the heavens only turned around the Pole Star because he observed them.

Accordingly in the present book I am a notch or two more cautious than in *After All*, for reasons which Wittgenstein has given. He was right to say that philosophy and religious thought should be centred about the problems of everyday life, problems that everyone is familiar with, and problems that theoretical physics really does not have any special bearing upon.

A friend, commenting, compares my self-renewing fountain with the Uroboros of mythology, the cosmic Snake that continually renews its own life by eating its own tail.

13. Objects and objections

According to empiricist philosophy, experience is our only source of knowledge; and according to much or most of classical British empiricism the data of experience are discrete particulars. 'All our perceptions', says Hume, 'are distinct existences'; and 'the mind never perceives any connexion' between them. Whatever things we can distinguish are as 'loose and separate' as if they had 'no manner of connexion'.

From these doctrines there developed the familiar Association-ist Psychology of the eighteenth and nineteenth centuries. Much as, according to chemists, material things are combinations of atoms and molecules, so in the mind simple sense-data are clumped together and combined to build up our mental model of the world. This analogy between the way the material world is itself composed and the way we compose our representation of it must have seemed very attractive; but it has an obvious major flaw. For when human experience is reduced to a staccato rat-a-tat-tat of particulars impinging upon the organs of sense, we have failed to give any account of time and the flowing biological continuity of our life.

William James tried to put this right. Medically-trained, he understood very well that a living organism's vital functions, brain activity, experience and so on have to be continuous. They cannot plausibly be analysed down to atomic events with voids between: some account needs to be given of the temporal flow of life. So in his early psychological writings James gives his classic descriptions of the Stream of Thought and of the self, and in his last writings he argues that our lived experience presents us not merely with particulars, but also with 'conjunctive relations' between them within the general continuity of personal experience. And this latter general continuity is seen in biological terms: it is a directly-lived continuity of life, of point of view, and of interest.

James goes on to attempt a biological account of our production of knowledge of the world around us:

> Knowledge of sensible realities thus comes to life within the issue of experience. It is *made*; and made by relations that unroll themselves in time.

But impressive though James' account is, he misses — or fails to make explicit — the role of language in forming experience and giving to it its flowing temporality. He gets within a hair's breadth:

> Philosophy has always turned on grammatical particles. With, near, next, like, from, towards, against, because, for, through, my — these words designate types of conjunctive relation ... (see *Essays in Radical Empiricism* 1912, pp. 41ff.)

But James doesn't see the next step in his own argument. He says that conjunctive relations are presented or given in experience, but does not see that the reason why they are presented is that experience itself is language-formed all the way down. Biological beings, we could not have pure, coherent and conscious experience *at all* unless language were already at work forming its elements, connecting them in various ways, and presenting them in flowing temporal succession.

The world of our experience presents itself, then, as a world already language-formed even in our first apprehension of it. This would in any case follow from our previous arguments showing that all our thinking is transacted in language – using the term in a broad sense to include not only natural language, but other systems of general signs as well. But now that we are speaking not just of our thought, but also of the world that presents itself *to* our thought, some additional arguments are worth adding.

First, it has long been recognized that all seeing is seeing-as; that is, that all perception is interpretative. We see, not just bare uninterpreted objectivity, but interpretations – things, states of affairs, *facts*. (*Facta*, Latin, are things *made*.) And indeed we use the word 'fact' to refer both to a true empirical assertion and to an actually-obtaining state of affairs. We do not distinguish very clearly between the two. We see that the book is on the table. We see the fact: the assertion, *that the book is on the table*, is what we see.

Secondly, any grammar-book will show how careful language is to prescribe the general structure of the world, a world of persons and things, of relations and qualities, of purposes and instrumental uses, in a framework of space and time. It's all there, in the parts of speech, the conjugations and the declensions. It cannot be that people first recognized these structures in their life-world and then invented analogous linguistic forms to track them, because they could never have come to a communal recognition of the structure unless they already had the linguistic forms. It must have been the other way round: social needs and the need to survive generated the linguistic forms, which were then successfuly imposed upon the life-world. Language has shaped the world, and not *vice versa*.

In this light we can view the sentence, with its subject-verb-object structure, as being already a little narrative. It is well-adapted, indeed, it was evolved so that it could be used to simulate, to describe or to prescribe a biological being's forms of interaction with the world of its life. And – harder to see, but more striking – the time of our life is an effect of, is produced by, the time of our language.

One thing is sure: there had to be cultural institutions that would help us survive and there had to be a life-world that we could inhabit, or we wouldn't be here now. And when William James emphasizes the facts that knowledge is knowing, that knowing is a temporal process, and that 'true' beliefs are beliefs that it is good for us to hold, he is urging us to forget the old domination of philosophy by the ideals of contemplative knowledge and of knowledge as a motionless mirroring of the world.

Rather, he is teaching us to see knowledge as a continuing communal activity whereby we constantly readjust ourselves to life, renegotiating our *modus vivendi* and retelling our own life-stories.

As used to be said of God, we know our world by making it – and, in our case, by continually remaking it.

Now, once it is fully understood both that our thinking is language-formed all the way down, and that the objective world is correspondingly language-formed all the way down, then mind-matter dualism is at an end. Your mind moves to the front of your face: the product of your (culturally-guided) thought is the ordered life-world of your daily experience. Your world is a reflection of what you are; you are the life you are living; you are the sum of your transactions with your milieu. You couldn't be more at home. It's your world.

However, there is a downside. We cannot fully grasp how completely at home we are here in this life, unless we have understood that everything that has been said requires us to give up for good the concept of substance. 'Substance' was independent real being, solid and enduring objective reality; and a good deal of Western thought has clung to substances – God, spirits, the soul, material substances. We have wanted to live in a stable and well-furnished universe.

But the vision of the world as a temporal flux of disseminating, scattering energies-read-as-signs blows away all traditional ideas of substance. Imagine that with a group of friends you are reading a play – perhaps *Hedda Gabler*. A play is a little world made only of language. But language brings along other things with it – feelings, social relations, actions and consequences. The member of your group who is reading Hedda's part gets interested, and tries to express the feelings that were (one may suppose) annexed by Hedda herself to her words. Joined up, these feelings become a mimesis or representation of Hedda's subjective life. She starts to become 'real' as a character.

'Real' – how real? When she has been conjured up, Hedda herself is still only an interpretation, a wraith hovering over the occasion. When the play is done she's gone, and nobody would trouble to ask where. A person is a dramatic effect produced over time: no more than that.

Is it any different with you and me? Remember, I have no inner core-self. I am merely an interpretation – my own interpretation, or perhaps someone else's interpretation – of the sum of my own expressive or communicative behaviour. It's not just a *fact* that there's nothing else to go on, but rather that nobody can say how there could possibly be anything else to go on. I might spend five years in psychoanalysis with Freud himself, but in the end Freud's knowledge of me would not and could not amount to anything more than an interpretation of the flow of signs on my surfaces – my yakking, my body-language. And an argument of the same general type can easily be framed to demonstrate that all substances – selves, or whatever else – are merely interpretations, transient constructs. Simmias was correct after all (Plato's *Phaedo*, 85c–86d).

A few moments ago I was trying to show that Heidegger and the rest were wrong. We are not 'homeless'. On the contrary, we are completely at home in this world of ours, and couldn't be more so. We are our world's and our world is us, ours. And now, secondly, it also follows that we are 'froth on the daydream', transient interpretations in a world of transient and scattering energies-read-as-signs – which news, be it understood, is supposed to make us feel not less happy, but still *more* so! Are you content to be a happy chance, felicitous froth?

This is a crux. On the one hand, in the Western tradition most people's orientation has long been objectivist. They have wanted objective norms in morality, objective truth in science, and knowledge of an objectively-real God in religion. We always seek to familiarize the world, that is, to make it like a comfortable and well-furnished house for us to inhabit, full of tangible property that makes us too feel that we are people of substance; and that in turn means that we build up around ourselves an unchanging framework of religious objects, timeless truths, moral and physical laws, immortal souls and all the rest. With half our minds we are aware that all these objects themselves have histories, being themselves merely transient cultural products: but we repress and we deny the obvious, clinging instead to our idols.

For every idea of objective reality and unchanging truth is an idol, a fetish, an illusion – and therefore a serious threat to our happiness. The true philosophical (and religious) happiness is to learn to float, to go with the flux, to say Yes to transience, to let go.

Why?

14. The first happiness: ecstatic immanence

What is the goal of life: what is the highest and greatest happiness a human being can attain? A very old tradition going back to Plato and Parmenides argues that since reason is the noblest part of our makeup, the supreme good for us must be a condition in which our reason is completely satisfied. And what most satisfies reason? The old philosophy answered: objective rational necessity of existence. So our reason is most completely at rest and satisfied when we contemplate, intuitively and not merely discursively, the luminous and self-evident necessity and perfection of the eternally Real.

In this doctrine about the Highest good, philosophy was long in agreement with monotheistic religion. Relogous doctrine described the Object contemplated as the divine essence, the contemplation of it as the vision of God, and the happiness which that contemplation will bring us as beatitude. As the Westminster Larger Catechism of 1648 puts it:

> Question 1. What is the chief and highest end of man?
> Answer.   Man's chief and highest end is to glorify God, and fully to enjoy him for ever.

But in those same years, the 1640s, an entirely contrary view was developing. The influence of Galileo's natural philosophy was leading some writers to portray human beings as physical systems in ceaseless motion, always restless and anxious:

> There is no such thing as perpetual tranquillity of mind, while we live here; because life itself is but motion, and can never be without desire, nor without fear, no more than without sense . . .

> No discourse whatsoever can end in absolute knowledge.
> (Hobbes, *Leviathan*, 1, 6 and 7)

Hobbes is plainly right. We are always inside our own biological life, a life which is always temporal and always involves an exchange of energies, and we are also always held within the mediacy and the relativities of the world of signs. Since nobody at all has ever had any other perspective upon the world, dreams of jumping right outside our biological life and right outside the world of signs are silly. We have not the least idea of where there could be to jump to, nor of how we could get there and yet still be ourselves.

Modern philosophy will therefore not seek our final happiness anywhere else but in the here and now, in this life and under the present conditions of existence. And it need not concern itself with every sort of happiness, but only with the happiness that can be gained with the help of specifically philosophical arguments. Which is a lot, because we have already found reason to reject the Leibnizian doctrine of metaphysical evil, the claim that there is something systemically wrong with the human condition. We will become happier if we are truly persuaded that our life is not blighted in the way people once supposed it to be.

The case is that, given that we are language-using beings (and how could it be otherwise?), there can be no reason to voice complaints about the conditions that make our linguisticality possible. In any case, what's *wrong* with time and society, plurality and finitude? We have no idea of how things might be otherwise. I have tried to show that the self, language and the world are all made of the same kind of stuff. We are not exiles, cut off or alienated from a True Home elsewhere; this world is our true home and our final world, with no further world beyond it. It is in a very strong sense *our* world, the product of our history and, both for good and ill, a reflection of ourselves; both a judgment upon us and also a challenge to change things and put them right.

Our world is in a very strong sense precisely adapted to our faculties, our needs and our capacities, not because somebody else made it so but because we made it so. Again, how could it be otherwise? Of course what we see lies within the spectrum visible to us, and what we hear lies within the range of sound audible to us. Nobody was needed to prepare the world to be a home for us, because, necessarily, we make it a home for ourselves.

It follows that there is no sense in the romantic pessimism of those philosophers who speak of us as having been 'thrown' into a world in which we now find ourselves abandoned and homeless. On this point Wittgenstein is surely right, as against Heidegger and Sartre. Because the human condition is radically outsideless there is no larger background against which we might set it in order to make global judgments about it. So there is no basis for saying that there is anything intrinsically wrong with our situation.

Because 'cosmic' discontent with the human condition is meaningless, we are most happy when we stop pretending that we don't really belong here, and learn instead to identify ourselves completely with the flux of our own life. We give up the idea that either truth or meaning or value can be anchored to any fixed points outside the flux of life, and we thus give up all 'absolutes' and notions of substance.

Hardest of all, this means giving up fixation. Freud, in a 1915 essay 'On Transience', asks why people have found the transience of flowers, of the summer and of life sad, and answers that human love always tends to become fixated upon its object. I am desperately afraid that the beloved object will die, pass away or abandon me, leaving me alone and lost. I find it especially hard to complete mourning and let the dead go. But this is absurd, says Freud. We should let time go by, and accept Nature's cyclical passing away and subsequent self-renewal. Would anybody in her right mind prefer a plastic daffodil that does not die to a real one that does?

So we should opt for short-termism, solar living, and love that does not cling or become fixated. All are valuable as correctives. Short-termism is valuable, because – like the late-mediaeval world which preceded it – the modern age constantly urges us to plan ahead, so that we end up spending far too much time and effort on attempts to secure our longer-term well-being. People become bond-servants, paying off their twenty-five-year mortgages and their forty-year pension plans.

Solar living is Georges Bataille's term for what I have elsewhere called 'Glory'. Bataille teaches that we should live as the sun does.

Its life, the process by which it lives, and the process by which it dies all exactly coincide. It believes nothing, it hasn't a care, it just pours itself out. Its heedless life-giving generosity is its glory.

Glory is a state of being wholly and unreservedly given to one's own life. The sun does it without a thought, but it's not so easy for us human beings. Fear and anxiety hold us back. We start looking for points outside the flux of life: anchors, guiderails, landmarks. Absolutes, certainties, substances – idols, one and all of them. Of these things-to-hold-on-to, the idea of the Self is one of the most important. We like to think that there is a Real Me, something enduring and self-identical that transcends the flux of life. However, for so long as we believe in any sort of fixed points outside the flux of life, we will be incapable of Glory and afraid of death. Life is outsideless, and glory means giving up all ideas of substance, of absolutes or of things outside time, and losing our Selves in the flux of life. One should be ardent, burning like a fire and burning out.

Everyone knows something of how blissful this can be, because everyone, or almost everyone, knows of something – it may be visual experience, or meditation, or productive work or music – which has the power to draw them out into total absorption. You cease to be a separate, self-conscious individual standing back a little from life, and find instead that you are taken right out of yourself and drowned in the flux of events. I call this ecstatic immanence, and it is utterly blissful.

An active version of the same thing shows itself when a person of action catches the crest of the wave and becomes completely joyous in, given to and identified with their task. Solar living is a state in which we have transcended the usual distinctions between gaining and losing, giving and receiving, living and dying. To live beyond the distinctions is 'eternal life'.

Thirdly, there is the question of whether we can learn a kind of loving which does not cling or become fixated. Traditionally, profane love has been regarded as relatively egoistic by comparison with sacred love and compassion, which (it is claimed) do not to the same extent single out particular objects and become attached to them. But in practice, surely, there is a pathology of sacred love as well as of profane. In both cases we are driven by the fear of death and loss, and cling to something that may perhaps deliver us from it – another person in the case of erotic infatuation, and our own immortal souls in the case of religion. So we become exclusively attached, either to another who can save us, or to some mechanism by which we hope to secure the salvation of our own souls.

Neither of these devices succeeds. The *egoisme à deux* of a great love comes to an end, and the attempts made in Christian doctrine to create within the believer an invincible confidence of personal salvation (by 'Assurance', by granting absolution, etc.) have failed. The only way to save one's soul now is to lose it – that is, to give up the belief that the Self somehow transcends its world. Truly we are happier without that idea.

15. Solar loving

In the West at least, a man will often find that he falls in love most deeply with the woman who most vividly – though usually unconsciously – reminds him of his mother. This new love, he discovers, has the power to console him for the loss of his first and greatest love because she reawakens, and provides a legitimate and socially-approved focus for, so much intense, painful buried feeling. Years ago, in order to become an independent heterosexual male, the young boy was obliged to renounce his mother and all that he felt for her. The age at which the break with the mother is formalized varies from one society to another, but it usually seems to take place at around six to eight years. His curls are cropped, his dress changes, and he is taken into a more masculine milieu. It is very hard: some males never quite make the emotional break, and others never quite recover from it. But an adult love seems to be a way of regaining the mother at one remove. His libido becomes fixated again, and he returns to the physical comforts – the kisses and cuddles – of childhood. Now he is liable to regress to infancy in a big way: he can become touchy, suspicious, jealous, possessive and anxious. He is deter-mined to have her all to himself, and he is terrified of losing her. In short, the mighty domineering patriarch is a thunderous return of the baby he once was. He achieves fulfilment as an adult male by again becoming overpoweringly wilful and demanding. In him, ironically, the most dominant human type coincides with the most dependent: the strongest and the weakest are alike in being the most *demanding*.

Interestingly, our religious history seems to tell the same story in reverse: in the Incarnation the Patriarch reveals his own true nature by becoming a child again. Yes, our psychosexual history and our religious history have each created the other. Around 27 to 29 centuries ago (that is, in the biblical scholars' terms, between J and the prophet Hosea) we learned to model all our piety on the relation to a capricious, demanding, jealous, overwhelming male Ego that must be waited upon with utter devotion. In relation to this stupendous Power, Israel was always a faithless, insufficiently-devoted wife or an erring child, always and irremediably in the wrong. It was not a very happy relationship.

Consider now the appearance of a truly sinless woman, a woman miraculously preserved from the taint of original sin, a woman totally and exclusively attentive, obedient and adoring, the woman whom the child in every man demands. Such a woman is Mary, and in her God is ready to become incarnate. She is really faithful. You have seen tens of thousands of images of Mary and paintings of episodes in her life: ask yourself if you have ever seen even one in which her mouth is open, in which she is laughing or speaking, or in which she is kissing her husband, or even just looking at him? Joseph is annihilated, as we realize if we try to imagine a painting in a Christian church which in some way pictures Mary as displaying affection for her husband. It would appear indecent, and people would demand its removal. In the ideal Holy Family, woman is seen only as Mother, and never as wife. Mary's arms can only ever embrace one male, her infant Son. He is always her only beloved, who always has her undivided attention. Other women such as Mary of Magdala may approach him, but he cannot respond to them. He is always and only his mother's Son, and he cannot possibly be seen in any other woman's arms. He is restored to Mary's arms as her helpless child again in his death. The *Pieta*, the final scene, completes this story of an absolute love.

Our first thought may be, 'Like Father, like Son'. But our

second thought is that Yahweh in all his raging power and eloquence was never able to attract such pure and exclusive devotion from Israel as Mary shows to her mute and helpless Babe in life, in death. The Patriarch has won our love at last by revealing his own inner weakness. And then again our third thought is that our whole religious tradition for a long time has centred upon the cult and the care of the male ego. The strange drama of its strength and its weakness, its demands and its threats, builds the world and orders society. For all its power, it is strangely unconscious and bewildered: it has to be tended, pampered, indulged and adored, waited upon hand and foot. The fragile Omnipotent, the bossy Babe, the vulnerable Male is all that the West has known of religion so far. Astonishing.

There is more yet: for having constructed religion in sexual terms we were sure eventually to return and reconstruct sex as religion. We transferred to human love the idea that we can achieve blessedness and immortality if only we can give a sufficiently whole-hearted and exclusive devotion to Another's needy ego. Salvation by absolute service, again – but now, in the human case, made *reciprocal*.

This happened amongst the courtly lovers of late-twelfth-century France. The ideal of pure Romantic love was surely indeed *egoisme à deux*, a dream of reciprocal idolatry in which each would be to the other both a perfect parent and a perfect child, both cherishing protector and devout worshipper. Each would be the other's only religion. They would give each other immortality.

So strange is this ideal that we cannot help but wonder at its former power. It derives from the image of the Madonna and Child. Mary's eternal Maker has become also her helpless dependent and she kneels to worship him in his weakness. Fine: but it also doubles this image, makes it two-way and thereby fatally overinflates it. Do we really want, my dear, to be each other's only god?

Today, when everyone who has studied theology has learnt that religion is purely human, with a purely human meaning, none of this is surprising. But none of it is really accessible to us any more, either. Because all the Western religions have been so overwhelmingly sexist and idolatrous for so long, virtually all

Westerners equate 'theological' thinking with phallogocentrism; with, that is, *das Männlichesprinzip*, the assumption that every aspect of Reality is traceable back to and founded in the decree of a single sovereign masculine will. Religion then becomes exclusive devotion to the service of One who is, in a male-ego sort of way, infinitely demanding: all-powerful, yet strangely needy. A Creator who also, as the Nativity shows, *needs to be mothered*. But the *Männlichesprinzip* is simply not tenable, partly because biologists now know that if one of the two sexes is primary and the other should be regarded as an aberrant, variant form of it, then it is the female that is primary and the male aberrant, and not *vice versa* as tradition mistakenly believed. The old appeal to nature in support of male primacy has backfired horribly.

(In a way, tradition also knew this: for didn't it say, didn't it know, that as everywoman makes a youth into a patriarch by making a baby of him, so Mary has accomplished the even greater feat of making the Eternal Patriarch into a helpless babe? Doesn't she, the Mother of God, therefore have the greatest power of all? The humanistic, Comtist, meaning of Christianity perhaps shows up here, because in popular religion God the Father – symbolized by Joseph – fades out, and Mary has become pre-eminent.)

But, secondly, the *Männlichesprinzip* is also untenable because modern philosophy cannot conceive how a solitary individual will could produce a world. Worlds are common, that is, they are public and communal productions, full of contrasts and oppositions. They are produced by intercourse and intersubjectivity, and in no other way. The whole idiotic (*literally* 'idiotic': it's the Greek word for what belongs to the private individual self) cult of the Ego must go. Getting rid of the belief in substance, we get free also of fixation, fetishism, clinging and the now-rather-repellent Western idea of romantic love as reciprocal ego-massage. Simultaneously blowing each other up like balloons! We reject that notion utterly, and replace it by what we may call 'solar loving'.

Solar loving is ardent and heedless. One should hope to go up like a rocket and burn out at the summit of one's flight, falling unnoticed to earth in the darkness. Solar loving, too, is free from all clinging and calculation. It idolizes neither its object nor its own abjection. It is not planning to achieve immortality. We lie about these things. We use the phrase 'till death do us part' as if it meant 'forever'; but it doesn't. On the contrary, the words are meant to remind us that all flesh is as grass and our time is very short. Sex is very close to death, and love, like time and joy, is winged. It flies.

This is what solar loving is like: it is easy, going. It burns ardently, it gives, it passes away. Its peculiar joy is of the kind I have called 'ecstatic immanence'. It is immersed in and unreservedly given over to its own utter transience. 'Glory', the only true eternity. Going, going, gone.

We should break free from the old equation of religiousness with the *Männlichesprinzip* and the quest for immortal selfhood. Instead, we have cosmic humanism, ecstatic immanence, glory.

16. Orange Tips

Wadloes Footpath, near Cambridge, is a narrow green lane between old and overgrown hedges. On a May morning in brilliant sunshine the young green of the vegetation still has a touch of yellowness in it, and is so bright that it seems to fluoresce. Male Orange Tip butterflies patrol up and down the hedgerows, looking at cow parsley and garlic mustard, searching for the females. The flash of colour on their forewingtips is a more brilliant orange than orangepeel itself. Occasionally they dip to drink briefly from the new bramble flowers, whose petals somehow contrive to be simultaneously as shinywhite as freshly-washed porcelain, as crinkly and fragile as India paper, and as soft as skin.

I stand still, to drink in once again the visual plenitude of the world. It seems almost supernatural. How does green get to be greener than green, like this? How does a butterfly's wingtip get to be so much more orange than any real orange can be, and how is this white whiter than white?

In the older literature such experiences of super-real visual plenitude were much discussed. People associated them with extravertive mysticism, with the use of certain drugs, with the work of certain painters (especially slightly mad ones like Van

Gogh), with poets like Gerard Manley Hopkins, with the onset of an epileptic seizure, and perhaps also with fifteenth-century French manuscript illuminatious such as those in the *Très Riches Heures* of the Duc de Berry. Because the experience was thought to be somehow 'supernatural', it seemed to be appropriate to read it as justifying a two-level world-view. Mere nature, by itself (and being, as we all know, only *mere*), could never get to be so brilliant and beautiful. What was happening on the footpath was that the natural light in which we ordinarily see things was being hugely reinforced, amplified, charged up and brightened by a distinct supernatural Light that in some ineffable way shines through the world and 'illuminates' it. So we see the world as Creation, new-minted from God's hand. Or we see the world as like a stained-glass window, lit up by the uncreated Light that shines through it. Yes, the world is only a veil: the real and eternal Beauty belongs not to it but to Something Else Beyond that it dimly reflects, or that shines through it.

The main intellectual objection to this analysis is that it is incoherent. The Supernatural Light has got to be pretty much the same kind of light as the natural light, if it is to enhance it and to make the orange in the Orange Tip's wing that extra-brilliant orange colour. But at the same time the supernatural Light has got to be metaphysical and quite different in kind from any merely natural light, in order to justify the two-level metaphysics. So the last paragraph seemed to make sense only because it muddled two profoundly different uses of the word 'light' – one being grounded in everyday visual experience and physics, and the other being derived from our philosophical and religious tradition.

The traditional Christian-Platonist interpretation of natural beauty was, then, profoundly confused. The beauty had to be *there*, both real and very striking, in order to call for explanation. But the explanation when proffered said that it wasn't really there at all. It was merely a refracted earthly image of the eternal divine Beauty that somehow shone through and brightened it up. The Supernatural Light was both enough like natural light to brighten up our human visual experience, and at the same time had to be totally different, because the divine Light and Beauty are invisible, intellectual, timeless and belonging to the eternal world.

If this account was intellectually a mess, what was morally repulsive about it was the way it insisted upon separating 'mere nature' from its own beauty. What a profound injustice; and what could be the rationale for such a move? I'm talking ecstatic immanence: I'm describing an experience of visual joy, plenitude and *solidity*. I'm not seeing the world as like a Venetian blind, between whose slats a little Light from Outside comes in. On the contrary, the world is very full and complete, and I feel profoundly at one with it. There is no reason for introducing any ontological split into the situation.

I add two supporting arguments. First, experiences of intense visual joy are now democratized, and may very well figure in the everyday experience of many perfectly ordinary people. They used to be thought extraordinary, or even 'wild' or mad, in such a way that their occurrence seemed to justify inference to a hidden supernatural Cause. Not any longer: our modern biological theory has not only immensely enriched the natural world and led us to look at it more closely, but it has also reminded us of the biological functions, both of bright warning coloration like the Orange Tip's, and of visual pleasure and visual signals in turning us on and making our juices flow. Thus a kind of visual joy that used to seem supernatural has now been explained, so becoming naturalized and therefore democratized – and a good thing, too.

Secondly, my experience on the footpath was not at all an experience of anything supernatural. It was rather an experience of ecstatic immanence, and above all of perfect unity and harmony between subjective experience, language and the objective world. Words like *green, orange*, and *white* might have been coined to describe just this fluorescent greenness, this flamelike orange and this porcelain white. My heart goes out, and I am ravished, in a moment when vocabulary, feeling-experience and the objective intensity of life's joyous self-affirmation all coincide so completely. Nobody in his right mind could ever want or imagine anything better than this. What else could the Unitive Vision be?

Note

To make one point more explicit, Orange Tips are so beautiful because they taste horrible, having eaten so much garlic mustard in their caterpillar youth. The colour that turns me on is there in order to turn predators off.

We use similar highly-luminescent colours to protect traffic cones, traffic policemen, and highway workers. Why don't I see *them* as beautiful?

17. The aims of life

In everyday conversation people make a distinction between what you are saying and what you 'really mean', or what you are 'driving at'. It's a very instructive distinction.

'What you say' is the stream of apparently harmless pleasantries that you are uttering. Your remarks are mild, courteous, even a little euphemistic. You certainly don't seem to be giving anything away, nor to be getting at anybody. But imagine that your interlocutor is an old friend, or a highly-suspicious parent or spouse with well-developed radar. In such a case the other party seems to regard anything you say as 'coded'.

Various idioms are used at this point. 'Behind' what you say is your 'hidden agenda', what you were really getting at, your subtext. You thought perhaps that you were 'playing poker', trying very hard not to betray yourself or give yourself away. You imagined that you were speaking quite innocently; but against your will some sort of *double entendre* or irony crept into what you said, or you let slip a clue of some kind, and your partner fastened upon it instantly. You can hide nothing from her – and, by the way, there is an interesting disagreement of interpretation at this point. You claim you were speaking quite innocently, whereas she assumes you were speaking in the kind of politician's code that all party members understand, and are intended to understand. The rules require one to seem to keep up appearances by using the conventional euphemisms, but everyone who is in the know has no difficulty in getting the message. It is clear to all present that the speaker intends to use a form that appears to conceal but will in fact reveal. The speaker knows he is speaking in a code that is understood. So now, to return to the domestic case, your partner reckons that despite your protestations of innocence you know perfectly well what signals you were sending out in what you said. What you pretend was harmlessly said, she knows was maliciously intended. You are in deep trouble.

And so it goes on: in a conversation between two suspicious old parties who have known each other for years, it will often be found that each replies not to what the other has actually said, but to what he or she takes the other to have been really getting at. Go on – listen to yourself. A conversation is a battle fought on more than one level at once, like three-dimensional chess, which makes it very difficult for a playwright or scriptwriter to write convincing dialogue. Dim critics used to say that Harold Pinter portrays a world in which people do not really communicate, but when he is acted well enough – as, for example, by his former wife Vivienne Merchant – he is perfectly clear. Between his characters there is not a shortage but an excess of communication, much of it murderous.

At this point people refer to the standard distinctions between appearance and reality, text and subtext, high life and low life, and the conscious versus the unconscious meaning of what has been said. But these simple binary contrasts are too crude: they are insufficient to account for the three or four levels upon which a conversation may be taking place, and they don't account for the pleasure we take in playing the different levels off against each other by using various devices of concealment and revelation; nor do they account for the pleasure we may take in receiving, as well as handing out, banter, chaffing, teasing, evasion and flirtation. Why is it, indeed, a kind of gesture of affection to subject someone to mock-sadistic teasing?

We take pleasure also in the extreme delicacy of the transitions that are made from one mode to another. For example, consider the sort of person of whom it is said that 'you don't know where you are with him'; 'I am not sure whether he is being altogether serious'; or, 'Is he being ironical?' Such a person may wish to tantalize by holding the situation in suspense. He relishes ambiguity and evasion – but the tiniest twitch of an eyelid may be sufficient to establish a mood of knowing complicity, and a word may change the mood again and bring the whole affair right out into the open.

What are we to make of these complexities? Our entire philosophical and religious tradition, almost with one voice, has deplored and ignored them. It has assumed that we are 'naturally', and wish to be, and should be, metaphysically unified persons whose communication with each other is straight, truthful and unambiguous.

Strange, that every human being who has lived with another knows perfectly well that language is incorrigibly duplicitous and so are people, and our life would be wretchedly dull if it were not so. But duplicity unfortunately has a dirty name. There has been a heavy ideological bias in favour of the unity of all truth, the unity of virtue, 'straight' communication, a unified life with one great aim, and a unified 'examined' selfhood, clear to itself, that wills only one thing.

Why? Our tradition, philosophical and religious, was largely written by single males who believed in one masculine God, and who praised all that was unified, independent and self-sufficient. Duplicity they associated with role-play in social life, and especially with Woman, who represented temptation to the philosopher and the saint alike.

In the older pre-philosophical and pre-monotheistic cultures, however, the notion of a plurality of souls in each human being was common. It accords with experience, and it accords with biology.

Mythically, we may picture the world as consisting of a great outpouring, flowing discharge of energies; even, a slow-motion explosion. But the world is not quite homogeneous. Around irregularities in the flux relatively-stable objects form, objects such as galaxies, stars, planets and organic molecules. Some of these objects are a little like eddies or whirlpools in the way that they preserve a more-or-less constant form by continually extracting energy from their environment, even though the material of which they are composed is continually changing. Thunderstorms, hurricanes and tornadoes are examples of such objects; but living things are by far the most striking. In their case the individual organism is very shortlived, but individuals have ways of producing replicas of themselves, and moreover with so many small variations that the whole line of descent can evolve and so can become very long-lived.

Now the Universe, as one might say, selects for longevity; but what is particularly striking about living things is that they have introduced into the world a far greater degree of variety and complexity than is to be found anywhere else. And why? Because, for the whole project of life to work at all, a living thing must be programmed with a group of slightly discordant aims. The list will differ from one species to another, but it is clear that in the case of highly-evolved social mammals the organism must in the first place secure its own survival. It will maintain a little coolness and detachment, a little space around itself, even when in a grazing herd. What is wild is therewith *farouche*, also a little skittish and shy. Secondly however, if it is one of those creatures that must co-operate in order to survive, it must communicate with other members of its own kind, building up a set of ritualized behaviours, and therewith the vocabulary of signs through which it establishes its social world. Thirdly, it must pass on its genes, and therefore it must communicate and co-operate very closely with a suitably-selected mate; and it must of course be ready to give its life for its young.

We can now return from our excursion into myth. We can now say that if indeed we have evolved from some such background as that, then it is not in the least surprising that living things in general, and we in particular, should behave in ways that reveal the simultaneous working of a number of distinct aims, or even sub-personalities. For example, in conversation with someone we may be maintaining a little polite caution, coolness, distance and privacy, whilst at another level probing to satisfy our curiosity, and checking out whether the other is friend or foe, one of us or not one of our sort. At a third level, we do enjoy communication, checking out the likeness and unlikeness of our usages, feeling-responses, values, opinions, world-view; and at a fourth level some kind of sexual enquiry and signalling may be going on.

Now we see why it is that in conversation we take pleasure in its multi-levelled character, the slightly discordant co-presence of various aims, the occasional establishment of sympathy or complicity, and flipping from level to level. The complexity here, the discordant interplay of different aims and of concealment and openness, is the play of life itself and is exhilarating – as well as being (no doubt) sometimes painful and difficult to resolve. It is our inner conflict that makes us intelligent, makes us conscious and makes us communicative – which raises a fresh question.

I mentioned earlier how difficult it is to write convincing modern dramatic dialogue. How do you pre-calculate all the nuances, the hints and ironies, the veiled menace, the possibilities of diverse interpretations, if indeed the things people say are as duplicitous as I've been arguing? And more than that, how did we ourselves manage to frame some of the crafty and malicious things we find ourselves insinuating? One may listen to working men chaffing each other at high speed for an hour or two, or one may listen to ambiguously flirtatious talk at a party, and one may wonder how people are able to find and calculate such wickedness so rapidly.

I have a double answer: the first is that the production of language is a rather more automatic process than most of us realize, and the second is the doctrine that 'the sign itself is a compromise-formation'. Signs, language and our other associated means of communication have been evolved by us precisely in order to be as forked, slippery and treacherous as they are. They are, naturally enough, as devious as we who made them.

Note

I once wondered whether Nietzsche's biological naturalism is compatible with his nihilism (*The Sea of Faith*, second edition SCM Press 1994, pp. 214f.) Wondering if my complaint rebounds against myself, I have used the word 'mythical' to describe the little narrative excursion above into our evolutionary background. Otherwise it might seem that I'm falsely pretending to go beyond the proper limits of language and narrative, and reintroducing a form of scientific realism.

However, biology is perhaps a special case, as Schopenhauer points out. For if we really are biological organisms ourselves, then we have purely immanent access to – that is, we have inside knowledge of – what it is like to be a biological organism. Thus, careful attention to the ways in which people communicate at a party might enable one to check out a whole lot of biological theory while remaining *strictly* inside the realm of signs. Which is obviously true.

When in this way a bit of scientific theory and a bit of literary theory connect up, the world begins to make sense. Hence the prominence of biology in the present work.

18. The sign as a compromise-formation

It has long been recognized that a single form of words may have several different levels of meaning. In mediaeval thought even God was supposed to have said four things at once in each line of scripture. Aquinas, and Dante following him (*Epistola* x, 140ff.), distinguished between the *literal*, the *allegorical*, the *moral* and the *anagogical* senses of the text.

However, they did not thereby intend to attribute any mixture of motives to God. Far from it. Rather they saw God as being in total control of language, as using it purely didactically, and as having chosen to give us a once-and-for-all revelation that would need to be read in slightly different ways in different contexts. Having decided then to communicate his saving truth to human beings in a text that is to remain authoritative, God has no problem at all in producing forms of words capable of meaning one thing in the time of Moses, and another to a later generation in the light of Christ; that mean one thing in relation to the moral life in this world, and another in relation to our attainment of final salvation.

Here the *multiplex intelligentia* is 'economic' and didactic; but in the case of our human utterance it is expressive. I can only produce one line of utterance at once, but I incorporate within myself several different and discordant voices, all of them trying to make themselves heard. The problem in all human expression – and, indeed, the reason why we talk all the time – is that through expression we are attempting to unify ourselves. We are trying to get it all together. We are comical creatures: we give ourselves away as plural, in our use of a style that fictions our unity.

Freud's contribution here in his idea that the neurotic symptom is always a compromise-formation. I may for example intensely desire to do something wicked and forbidden, and I may also feel a great need to punish myself for wanting to do something so wicked. Or I may feel a great need to be purged of some past sin, but open confession of it may for some reason be out of the question. In such cases, Freud suggests, the neurotic symptom may arise as a compromise that solves my dual problem. It is a piece of symbolic behaviour through which I can simultaneously both gratify my wish and punish myself for doing so.

Freud and his followers have of course recognized that the principle here is of wider application. Indeed, it is a mainstay of the British way of life: the more solidly respectable people are, the more they enjoy scandal – especially, prurient tut-tutting gossip about prominent people's sexual misdemeanours. They hugely relish both some vicarious participation in the sin and also their own direct participation in its punishment.

I take this admirable idea a stage further by holding that it applies to the sign and communication generally. It seems that we are complex biological systems that incorporate a number of sub-systems – even, sub-personalities – all of which are noisily clamouring for expression. Like the cosmos at large, like a Roman candle firework, the self is an outpouring of energies. If I believed in the Ego (and I'm not sure that I do) I'd say that the Ego is and has to be a politician. It has to find forms of words that will paper over the cracks, relieving a variety of different pressures, and satisfying a variety of different interests simultaneously. Through what we say we are trying to hold ourselves together; we are trying to weave ourselves into some kind of manageable unity (and in many cases, no doubt, with only very moderate success).

We can now understand the role of the sign in resolving conflicting motives. Imagine a grazing animal that suddenly detects a flicker of movement near it. Its problem can be represented in the form of a decision-tree, with a series of dilemmas that need to be resolved, one after the other. Is this a predator? If so, flight: if not, continue. Is it of some other species? If so, disregard it: if not, continue. Is it of the same sex, or of the opposite sex? If it is of the same sex, does it present a threat? Is it a rival or competitor and, if so, is it bigger than me, or smaller? Do I respond with flight, or with aggression? Turning to the other branch, if the approaching beast is of the opposite sex, is it available and is the time of year appropriate? If yes and yes, go into courtship mode; if no, disregard it.

As soon as we set out such a decision-tree in detail, we see how common and how biologically basic are situations of choice in which an organism is suspended, between the most intense arousal or anxiety leading to a fight-or-flight response on the one hand, and proceeding calmly to the next step in the analysis on the other. It is clearly highly stressful to the organism that it should have to live all the time at the very highest state of alertness, ready to flee or to fight for its life at a fraction of a second's notice. The entire species will find life much easier if individual animals can signal their status to each other, and can resolve their anxieties and their dilemmas by performing rituals that confirm everyone's status and move social relations on to the next stage.

There is no need to go into further detail: suffice it to say that the sign was first used in situations of the most extreme ambivalence. Its function is still to contain, to manage, to relieve and to resolve. Its use gets a highly-sensitive creature through the stresses and conflicts of its life – which, by the way, helps us to see how in psychotherapy 'the talking cure' works.

Secondly, this simple biological background story explains a second feature of the sign, which is that for any species its whole sign-vocabulary adds up to an inventory of its world. Hastily, one must add that this is an inventory of a very specialized kind. It is an intensively-emotive, behaviour-oriented inventory of the features of its world that are of urgent life-and-death importance to it. A living organism such as an antelope sees the world always and only from the point of view of its own interest in life.

An even more important point is the following: from its sign-vocabulary and ritualized behaviours we can reconstruct the antelope's world-view – and it is a 'public' world-view, in being common to all members of that species. Being living animals ourselves, we can reconstruct it and enter it imaginatively. So we can easily work out just what it's like to be an antelope.

In an article called 'What Is It Like To Be a Bat?' (*Philosophical Review*, 1974; reprinted in his *Mortal Questions*, Cambridge 1979) the American philosopher Thomas Nagel maintained that there is indeed something special that it is to be a bat, something we can never share. Nagel, in short, believes that there is something special called consciousness or subjectivity, which exists in different forms and is private.

I'm saying Nagel is wrong. A young antelope acquires the antelope-mode of consciousness by being inducted into, and appropriating, the antelope-vocabulary of signs and behaviours. (And I will allow that some of its vocabulary may be genetically-inbuilt.) The outer face of that same antelope-language is the objective world that antelopes inhabit. So that when in childhood we acquired a language, we acquired with it both an objective world and, subjectively, a mode of consciousness. 'To be conscious' *equals*, therefore, 'to have learnt a language'; which *equals*, 'to participate in some communally-evolved construction of the world and way of life'. If you are trading the signs back and forth with your neighbours, then you're in the world and you have the form of consciousness. The two ideas, that mind and matter are different realms, and that mental life is private, can both be forgotten. They are mythical.

During the half century or so since Wittgenstein wrote the famous comment, 'If a lion could speak . . . ', the study of animal behaviour has advanced astonishingly. My point is that today the study of a particular species' behaviour is very like learning a language. Animals do have what deserve to be called cultures, and rituals. There is even cultural diversity within a single species – for example, amongst killer whales, where hunting tactics like 'beaching' to catch seal pups are learnt, practised and transmitted within some descent-groups and not others.

Thomas Nagel tried to make things easier for himself by choosing bats, which have sense-organs we lack, and whose behaviour was not well understood twenty years ago. So he argued that a bat surely does have an angle on the world and it's an angle we cannot share; so that there is indeed something special that it's like to be a bat, and it's something private. In which case behaviourism must be wrong, and mind can't be eliminated.

I say Nagel's wrong, because he has not seen the difference that the discovery of language has made to the behaviourist's case. In the case of bats just as much as that of antelopes, there is no reason in principle why a student of animal behaviour should not learn everything there is to be learnt about the bat's way of life, sign-system and its ritualized behaviours. Everything the student learns is learnt by applying biological principles in order to understand how this bit of behaviour or that sign serves the interests of life. When the student has learnt and understood the whole life-language of battery (batdom?), then she knows just what it's like to be a bat and Nagel's question is answered.

Which recalls a point made earlier: the fact that we are ourselves living things who must see the world (*equals*, build our world) from a biologically-conditioned and interested viewpoint may limit our knowledge in some respects – but there are also a few directions in which it helps a lot. In myth and in hagiography it used to be dreamt that saints might understand the languages of animals: I'm saying that, if we but get the philosophy right, we will be able to recognize that we are now fulfilling that dream. And perhaps one day imaginative writers will be stirred to write children's books about animals that respond imaginatively to the new scientific knowledge.

We have been explaining the doctrine that 'the sign is a compromise-formation' like a Freudian neurotic symptom, by saying that the biological *Sitz-im-leben* (setting-in-life) in which animal signing has arisen is very tense, fraught and ambivalent. Signing helps the animal to contain its conflicting drives, resolve its dilemmas and negotiate its relationships. In our own case, so great is our need to communicate, and so hard do all our systems press forth into expression, that we spontaneously pour out language of great complexity, without precalculation. We should not be surprised, therefore, that deconstructive analysis reveals the presence of sharply conflicting forces at work beneath the surface of a text. *All* language has something of this character, I suggest, for very ancient biological reasons.

Because it must contain and manage conflicting forces, language has to be elastic. Our forms are elastic: listen to questions, in the home or in Parliament, and notice how a question is seldom just a question: it is rather a piece of flattery, a 'planted' 'feed', a complaint, a cry for help, a trap, an opportunity, and so on. Even more extraordinary is the variety of associations surrounding the words for certain persons and animals that are very close to us and that become lightning-conductors for our emotions. Anyone who takes an emotive-expressive view of language will be impressed by the case of the dog. It gets a barrage from every angle. Just think of man's best friend, of faithful hounds, and of Victorian dogs as 'curates in fur'; think of gay dogs and dirty dogs, dog days and dead dogs; of lucky dogs and lazy dogs, of a dog's chance and of dog eat dog, of a dog in the manger, dull dogs, surly dogs and the black dog, of a dog with a bad name and of the doghouse, of sleeping dogs, of the dogs of war and of dying like a dog, of lame dogs and a dog's life, of being dog-tired and lying doggo. At one extreme the idioms carry suggestions of affection, liking and respect; at the other extreme they suggest our contempt for a creature whose fate is wretched – and don't add, *sotto voce*, 'like ours'. The dog is the nigh boor, the fellow-creature: it may attract any, or several, of the whole gamut of emotions that we may feel for a fellow-human, ranging from the highest admiration and respect to the greatest scorn and disgust. And for the sake of honesty and truth it has to be added that a similarly wide and ambivalent range of associations shows up in the stock idioms used in the past when people spoke of Christ, and of woman. Woman, for example, is pictured by our inherited sexist idioms both as being gentler, purer and more virtuous than man and also as being relatively more fickle and even (at times) ritually unclean. Other creatures share the same ambivalent mix of associations: the domestic pig is a byword both for lovability and for dirtiness, and the cat both for calm cuddliness and for female ferocity.

Thus language expresses, manages, relieves and reconciles our divided condition: but by doing that it also does more. It lights up and finishes the objective world, as we shall see.

19. The religion of life

By assembling its whole vocabulary of cries, visual signals, scents, symbolic behaviours and so on, I have argued, we can gain access to an animal's world. It is a 'public' world, because it is common to all members of the species that use this vocabulary, but it is scarcely a cosmos. It is too fragmentary for that. Rather, it is a very selective vocabulary constructed with one and one only interest in view: the animal's interest in life. An animal must survive and reproduce, and to that end it needs to co-operate with others of its kind. It has no purely speculative interest; its vocabulary is quite ruthlessly practical. And in this respect the form its interest in life takes reminds one of a religion.

The analogy is this: just as the scope of an animal's vocabulary and its 'world-view' is strictly determined by one interest only, namely its interest in life, so (according at least to various Lutheran and existentialist theologians, following Kierkegaard) the vocabulary, the world-view and the practice of religion should be strictly determined by one interest only, namely the individual's interest in gaining *eternal* life.

In both cases a single overriding practical concern generates an entire vocabulary and way of life: in both cases we are concerned not with speculative truth but with practical truth. Animals, it seems, are the best existentialists. They are not concerned with knowledge just for its own sake. Instead they are committed in pure practical immediacy to a religion of life, very much as the existentialist believer, following Jesus' teaching about the birds of the air, seeks to achieve pure immediacy in commitment to a religion of eternal life.

A number of the oldest themes of human thought join hands at this point. In different ways, almost every age has deplored human dithering and anxiety and has looked to animals as moral emblems and as examples of how to live intensely and immediately. And, also in different ways, almost every age has believed that the further you go back into human history – Iron Age, Bronze Age, neolithic, palaeolithic – the more religious things get. Astonishingly, in East and West alike, both before and after the Enlightenment, people have usually supposed that there was a founding primal religious unity of all human life and thought. During the course of human history a long process of disintegration and secularization has exiled us from our origin; but even modern progressives, who are glad to have left Eden for a more diversified world, may still look back nostalgically to the Golden Age at the beginning. It was called 'paradise', the garden, and we still seek to recreate it in our modern gardens. Running water, birds and animals always figured in it, but my present suggestion is that after Darwin we moderns are perhaps beginning to see animal consciousness as *itself* the archaic, paradisal, unified, sacred mode of consciousness from which human history and civilization have exiled us.

Consider: as we lost Eden, we began to replace it with the Wilderness, now seen as the sacred world, unspoilt, virginal and holy. Sir David Attenborough, taking us to it, speaks in a breathless whisper. He is on holy ground. We may have lost Adam and Eve, but we are more than recompensed by the sight of him playing with gorillas. In the culture of childhood the former sacred world of divine beings, spirits and saints has been largely replaced by the animal world. Vegetarianism spreads apace, and animal charities, campaigning organizations and pressure groups flourish.

These phenomena may be regarded as signs of an emergent religion of life. Another is the fact that of the 65–90% of the population who in the advanced countries profess to believe in God, around half opt for a description of God as a 'life-force', rather than as a distinct supernatural Person in the older style. In short, they are opting for the sort of shift in religious thought that can be seen occurring in the post-Darwinian generation of writers – in such figures, that is, as William James, Henri Bergson and D. H. Lawrence.

I am not commending the religion of life here. The blind raging tenacious will-to-live certainly produces beautiful and moving effects; but it is morally wrong to plunge into reckless and total self-identification with it – as happened in the Nazi reading of Nietzsche, and (one fears) in some passages of Lawrence. From the point of view defended in this book, those who try to escape from language and reflection into pre-rational immediacy and pure biological force are pursuing an illusion. No immediacy outside language is accessible, and the will-to-live is not a thing-in-itself outside of and prior to language, that we can tap into 'pure', and live by. Those who think they have found it have in fact made a dreadful error. They have handed themselves over to an all-too-human *ideology* of force and power-worship.

My argument is very different: see for example '10. Cosmic humanism' above. I am an aestheticist. In contemplating Nature we are not looking away from language and humanity. Far from it: on my account the world we see is always *our* world, a language-formed and familiarized world. And that applies to the sky, the sea and landscape, as well as to townscape. Certainly, animal life has a special significance for us, because animals, sharing our biological make-up, and using signs to communicate with each other, live a life to which we can gain some access, and which we can view as a reduced version of our own. But it doesn't in the least follow that we should live like animals. On the contrary, our world is a human world. And because to us it is the objectified universal human over against us, poetically a Christ out-there, we can find in it our objective redemption. How? We'll see.

Note

For the sake of clarity and explicitness, an important general point needs to be made here. Throughout our tradition a contrast is drawn between the thing as it appears to us, the thing in representation, the thing as packaged in words and symbols and therefore known only *discursively* – and the thing as it really is, in itself and therefore one day perhaps to be known *intuitively*.

In their desire to draw this contrast, St Paul and Plato are at one. St Paul contrasts seeing 'through a glass darkly' with seeing 'face to face', as Plato contrasts seeing shadows on a wall with being able to look directly at the Sun: and it has been left to us mean-spirited moderns to point out that both of them are still firmly inside language and still using metaphors, even as they purport to be telling us about a level of knowing that altogether transcends language and metaphor.

Our present point is that so deeply engrained is the desire to establish the discursive/intuitive, phenomenal/noumenal contrast that it keeps recurring in modern philosophies of life and of the will, from Schopenhauer onwards. But it is objectionable, and even dangerous.

We must look for a philosophy (and a religion, too) that has finally given up the wish to go beyond language. Neither philosophy, nor theology, can get beyond metaphor (= the discursive level, the level of *Vorstellung* or Representation). Why do people still hanker after the illusion of transcendence? Isn't it obvious that there is no non-linguistic philosophizing or theologizing?

Non-realism then means an end to hankering after a Beyond, a Depth of things, 'a spiritual dimension', and being content with all this that we have around us. Hence my terminology of ecstatic immanence, solar living and glory.

20. The second happiness: the world as our objective redemption

Philosophers are usually people who prefer to lie low, avoid publicity and write in some learned code. With good reason, because people don't like them, suspecting that philosophers believe nothing, deny reality and think that life is but a dream.

When you were young, you learnt what 'the real world' is. Successful older relatives would lecture you about it. It was the largely masculine world of competition and power-struggles, and especially the world of finance and industry in which they had prospered. 'Learning to live in the real world' meant learning to throw oneself wholeheartedly into the game, accepting its rules as laws of nature. One may define Reality as that body of highly questionable customs, prejudices and assumptions which some group of people lives by and which they intend shall remain unquestioned. Realists are those excellent and virtuous folk who fit in, accepting the system and causing no trouble. They loyally and uncritically play the game, by treating a local set of human conventions as sacred objective realities, that must not be questioned or changed. The laws of the market are laws of Nature; the pronouncements of some assembly are immutable dogmas; the intuitions of 'commonsense' are eternal verities.

Philosophers are unfortunate misfits who can not quite go along with this: they just can't help seeing that all these 'objective realities' and 'eternal verities' are only human conventions. They also think that what human beings first invented, other and later human beings can modify, or even reinvent altogether. The American Constitution has been amended, and even the Laws of Cricket have been amended. Perhaps the Christian creed, and (the last taboo) even capitalist economics might not be sacrosanct. This last and truly *horrifying* thought shows why it is that philosophers are so often regarded as being both mad, impractical dreamers who deny reality, and also dangerous unpatriotic subversives who corrupt youth.

It all makes an unpropitious background against which to urge that philosophy now needs to be democratized. But the project has been attempted before. In their different ways, Jesus, Marx and the Buddha all say that we should not take 'the real world' for granted. It is passing away, says Jesus; if we over-objectify the world we over-objectify, and then become the prisoners of, our own ways of thinking, says the Buddha; the present order of things is an ideological fiction used to sustain unjust social relations, says Marx. And is it not the case that every great religious or political movement must assail the machinery by which the present order of things is made to seem unchangeable?

So I'm trying to democratize non-realism. It will turn out to be liberating where it helps people to question things that need to be questioned, and to set about remaking things that need to be remade; but (and this is a distinct point) it may also become a source of extraordinary joy and happiness.

The point is hard to see, because most of us are still traditionalists. We don't like critical thinking. We prefer to be held firmly within our local version of 'reality', such as in Britain is called down-to-earth, practical, 'hard', no-nonsense, straight-up-and-down, honest-to-goodness, commonsense 'basics'. But consistently critical thinking dissolves all this away like smoke, to produce the effect I call non-realism: the world suddenly seems very plastic, perspectival, a human construct and open to re-shaping. Inevitably, the initial reaction of traditionalists is one of alarm. They detest the thought that the rules might be changed, and they deride any suggestion to that effect as dreamy, visionary, up-in-the-clouds, airy-fairy and impractical.

All the metaphors suggest that when we leave traditional realism we exchange a solid world for a world made of clouds. So people's first response is fearful and hostile. But suppose that one came to see that all those solidities were merely effects of human ignorance, sin and anxiety, and of the self-interest of the powerful ones who control the persuasive metaphors by which we live? In that case, to be delivered from a reality grown old, oppressive and deeply corrupt might be a cause of rejoicing. And, by the way, it is also liberating to get into the habit of noticing that much of what passes for 'argument' in these matters amounts to no more than the repetitive urging of persuasive metaphors. Received practice is always pictured as being hard fact on solid ground; proposals for change are always pictured as misty dreams.

It is important to grasp how deep the argument cuts here. After the great nineteenth-century thinkers, many or even most of us may be ready to concede that *we* made the cultural world, *we* made the social order and *we* made the moral order, so that in principle everything in the human world is open to review, redesign and reconstruction. So far, so good: but now, what about the natural world? That is surely an entirely different matter, because we have always thought that the physical world exists independently of the language in which we describe it and the senses through which we apprehend it. And this historic assumption of ours is confirmed by both theism (which describes the physical world as having been created by God before ever we came into being) and natural science (which brackets out human subjectivity and constructs theories of the world as it may be relied upon to present itself to an ideal, disengaged observer). Both natural science and theism fiction a kind of *ideal* realism: they are allies, and neither of them understands, or can understand, or will ever be able to accept, the actual situation, which is that so far as we humans know for sure there has never been (and perhaps never can be) any other angle upon our world except our own. We simply do not have and cannot get the sort of independent validation that realism would require. We humans have always been inside our own biological lives and have only ever seen our world from within our own biologically-interested angle upon it. And there is no other angle. The only world we have, the only world we know anything about, and the only world we have the slightest reason to believe in, is the world of us talking animals, the world as it relates to, and is going to be seen by, beings with our needs, our purposes, our feelings and our language. The only 'reference group' that might be thought to be available for purposes of comparison consists simply of other animals. But, as we've noticed earlier, what makes them available is the fact that they are so like us; and by the same token, their world-views are even more tightly constrained by their own biological make-up than ours is by ours – not to mention their very much smaller vocabularies. The upshot of this is that, although animals are in a very special way accessible to us, they are so only by virtue of being in effect reduced versions of ourselves. They fit into *our* world, but they cannot give us a fully independent angle upon *the* world.

Remember that we argued earlier that our world is shaped all through by our language? The consequence is that if we are to conceive of any other angle upon our world that is truly an angle upon *our* world, then we have to conceive of that non-human observer of our world in anthropomorphic terms and as being a user of our language. So our extra-human witness becomes human again, after all. Being what we are, we can't help anthropomorphizing: there is no other morph. And that is what we in fact find: God is pictured as a user of human language who sees the same world that we see, and the ideal scientific observer who writes scientific papers also, just like God, talks our human language and observes the sensory qualities of things just like us. In fact, we don't imagine and we can't imagine either God or the ideal scientific observer as being genuinely independent of us. That is why the realism of theism and of natural science is and cannot possibly be more than, an ideal realism, a humanly-fictioned realism, heuristically or pragmatically useful and valuable to us humans for various of our human and practical purposes, but utterly irrelevant to philosophy. Philosophy – and perhaps it alone – can try, has to try, to stay with our actual condition, which is that we don't know, cannot know, will never know, and can have no reason to believe in, any other angle upon our world and our own lives except our own. We are talking animals, who must co-operate and therefore communicate. We have evolved complex habits – conventions – that govern our production of signs. Through our signs we differentiate, scale, grid, form, fix and publicize our own biological feeling-responses. Thereby we have constructed our common world – our world being made of our word-formed feelings, systematized by socially-evolved conventions.

And it is therefore, and could hardly *not* be, a radically human world. All the *qualia*, the feeling-tones of things – colours, tastes, smells, auditory pitches and tones, feelings of warmth and cold, hardness and softness, wetness and dryness – are human. They are our own feelings, scaled, fixed, projected out and formed into a common world by language. Because? – because not only the *qualia*, but also our construction of time and space, of motion and rest, of cause and effect, of thinghood and agency and so forth is also our own, and grounded in our own biological being. Thus the world that we see out there is the concrete universal humanum, our own objective reality as we have so far developed it.

For good – and ill. The Other over against us, which we contemplate and which calms and heals us, is sometimes an idealized version of ourselves, an image of our own redemption. This is clearly the case when we contemplate religious images, or a beloved person, or natural scenes or works of art. But more: a person who has been fortunate enough to have had a good early visual education can find the contemplation even just of *the visual field itself* salvific. Something similar is true of people who are highly musical, I'm told: but for the present it is sufficient to stress – against most of our philosophical and religious tradition – the pure and intense happiness that sense-experience can give. If you are fortunate, language can give you that same happiness, too. Our conflicts and our needs drive us to cry out to others, and thereby to produce our world, in which we contemplate our own accumulated expression, and which can give us the most complete satisfaction imaginable.

Further: the Other over against us may also, as a reflection of us, be a judgment upon us. The conflict, evil and pain that we contemplate appears to us as the objectification of conflict, evil and pain within ourselves. But here, for the first time, we see why the Good Friday preacher urges us to look at the image of the Crucified and say to ourselves, 'I did that'. For to learn to look at the world as our own expression is also to have learned a skill of confession, which is also salvific. To have learned to take upon oneself the evil in the world, as the objectification of evil that is within ourselves, is to have learned the truly universal and disinterested total compassion of which religion speaks.

In traditional Western thought the world was inevitably less perfect than its infinite Creator. But, perversely again, we are here stating the opposite view, so that we face the question: How come that the physical world around us is such a big improvement upon us, its makers?

Let me recapitulate the argument. We are complicated, divided creatures, systems with many subsystems whose aims are often divergent. Scientific theory pictures the Cosmos as a slow-motion explosion, and we ourselves are like slow-motion explosions, not static systems but burning, continually striving to express ourselves and to achieve our often-conflicting aims. To do this we must co-operate and we must communicate. Battling to get ourselves out into expression, communication, co-operation, we generate language – and at this point I have introduced the doctrines (a) that the sign itself, every sign, is like a Freudian compromise-formation. It is an expressive symbol that resolves the conflicting impulses of the sender who is producing it; and (b) that language is therefore inevitably, rightly and *redemptively* duplicitous.

Has it ever struck you that the body is a democracy? In our utterance our whole being is striving to express itself – not just the dominant (socially-disciplined, respectable) system, but all the subsystems as well. We don't have to think what to say; somehow, willy-nilly, it all comes out. We are such compulsive communicators that we always say too much. We betray ourselves, and must do so. And other people, being equally complicated themselves, have no difficulty at all in picking up and responding to all the overtones and the undercurrents in what we say. And my argument is that this feature of language is a good thing and not a bad. Throughout our tradition, from the Bible and the Greeks through to T. S. Eliot's *Four Quartets* ('Burnt Norton', V) writers have bemoaned the treacherousness of language, and have suggested that if we were completely rational or perfectly holy or both we would say only a little and always talk perfectly straight. 'The Government of the Tongue' was a favourite topic for preachers. But that whole tradition was mistaken, for it is a matter of our daily experience that you and I can only get ourselves together and express ourselves, you and I can only do justice to our mixed feelings and mixed opinions, by speaking always ironically, sarcastically, obliquely, teasingly, half-inquiringly, ambiguously, humorously, self-deprecatingly, knowingly, mockingly, insinuatingly and so on. We always speak with forked tongues. Even as we 'enter into the spirit of the thing', we show that we are aware that in every transaction of life we are but 'playing the game'; and the very consciousness that it is but a game only enables us to enter into it with the more relish. And what we relish is precisely the objective integration of our subjective discordance. We achieve at least objective wholeness in and through our self-expression. In what we produce we are more unified than we can ever be in ourselves.

Just as there is no subjective immortality, so too there is no subjective redemption. However far you go in religion and however hard you try, there will always be some emotional discord and some conflict of aims between the various subsystems in your biological make-up. Our subjective life is tragic, even for the holiest of all. In Christianity the central symbol of this is the Agony in the Garden, one of the supreme subjects of Western art. But we argue that objective redemption *is* attainable, and is obtained through language and through work as we express ourselves. Poetry, yes; but also just talk. Art, yes; but also manual labour, craft work and professional work.

We have in our culture a number of ideas of job-satisfaction, art therapy, and personal fulfilment through work. I am offering the following explanation of these ideas: because of the multivalence of signs and symbols, we are often able to contemplate in our own objective self-expression a synthesis and a wholeness that we will never be able to achieve within ourselves. Anything, anything whatever, that is said well or done well may give that happiness. We can achieve objective salvation and make our selves by pouring our hearts out and dying into our work. The notion that we can become our selves by keeping ourselves to ourselves is a mistake; we need to lose ourselves in order to become ourselves.

The next step in the argument is to understand the sense in which art produces nature. The starting point is this: the capacities that we call sight, hearing, speech and so on are not uncomplicated natural endowments, but culturally-acquired and culturally-guided skills. Notice here how the verb *to tell* is rightly used to mean both *discern* or *discriminate*, and also *spell out* or *put into words*. Prior to culture, we might experience visual stimuli, but there would be no conscious seeing, because we wouldn't be able *to tell* what we can see. It is by acquiring language that we learn how to tell what we are looking at.

In brief, there is a whole complex invisible apparatus by means of which we are able to put a construction upon raw sense-experience and build a world out of it. For Plato, this hidden apparatus was a transcendent order of ideas or intelligible essences. Kant changed it into a transcendental order of *a priori* concepts, 'transcendental' meaning, so to say, 'inwardly presupposed'. Kant claimed to be demonstrating by a kind of regressive analysis how we must build our world. But now, since Kant's time, we have come to recognize that the hidden apparatus by means of which we put a construction upon our experience is simply culture, working in particular through language. It is no longer *a priori* in the old sense. It is a kind of social programming. It has a history, it is somewhat different in different societies, and it slowly changes.

Here is the meaning of the past two hundred years: what God was, culture has now become. In the Christian era, Plato's World of Ideas was all enclosed within the mind of God. Looking at all things bright and beautiful, the Christian saw a world that had been formed by God's hand and in accordance with the divine Ideas. The Christian saw creation, a world already transformed from chaos to cosmos. The Kantian, a transitional figure, saw a world that became cosmos in and through his seeing of it. And then with Hegel the strange transformation of God into culture began. The process was cleverly masked, not least because the word *Geist* bridges the gap between God and culture so neatly, but the proof that it is happening is the growing importance of aesthetics. The poet becomes the 'unacknowledged legislator of the world'; and painters, by changing the way we see, embellish the world itself, so that to this day English people (for example) still see their own landscape through John Constable's eyes. The way painters actually make the world itself more beautiful is neatly brought out by the phrase, 'It's as pretty as a picture'. Painters gradually work upon us to make our visual sense as powerfully transformative as their own.

What God was, culture now is: it is that within us which makes the world intelligible and therefore beautiful, that in which we live and move and have our being. Where a local culture is threatened people will rally to it, and we may see the transformation of religion into 'ethnonationalism' and 'fundamentalism'; but more important is the fact that on the larger scale Western technology, Western video and audio culture, and Western science are now triumphing over the whole world, giving the whole world one world-view. We are all going Hegelian. The world has become so astonishingly beautiful because we now look at it through the eyes of such an army of scientists, painters, cameramen, book-illustrators, designers and many others. It is so utterly ravishing that it is able to deliver us from ourselves and to persuade us that in spite of everything the human enterprise is worth having been a part of. The world itself is our objective redemption.

Note

There is a difficulty for my argument in the extent to which a popular form of culture-pantheism has already become the de facto religion of the advanced countries. It is 'the return of the Middle Ages' (Eco); its imaginary world is 'the mediascape' (Baudrillard). Its chief institutions are the mass media, and its professionals the media folk, designers and trendsetters who define the *Zeitgeist* – seen, especially, as a *style* – and aestheticize all products accordingly.

This is a highly charismatic religion, in the sense that its leaders are those people who come to be perceived as, for the moment, embodying the *Zeitgeist*. Consider the list of celebrities (politicians, entertainers, actors, designers and so on) who are taken to define the Sixties – and note their standardized, mediaeval-type iconography, as fixed by Andy Warhol and others.

The prophets of the *Zeitgeist* are the trendspotters, and its theologians those influential columnists and culture-theorists who define the spirit of the age. The congregation for this religion consists of all the people who consume the output of the mass media, which means everybody, and above all those who market any kind of product: novelists, clothing manufacturers, composers, politicians, providers of services. All products have to be designed to please in the marketplace if they are to be successful. We learn what will please by studying the media, and being formed by them like everyone else. So this form of popular culture-pantheism has become an economically, and politically, compulsory religion.

This is a strange business. Culture is the immanent god that now prescribes our form of rationality, our world-view, our values, our tastes, and therefore our consumer choices. But its spirit is so capricious and volatile that nobody knows why it moves as it does. Astrologers, think-tanks, futurologists are hired, but to no avail. Media folk debate who's in and out, who's attracting attention and who is now unnoticed, who's coming up and who's fading. But why? Why did Margaret Thatcher's reputation and achievement look so invincible and then collapse so completely, within the space of four years?

We haven't a clue, and the philosophical and religious Right, with their objective standards and immutable Truths, will be quick to point out that my own thoroughgoing culturalism and relativism goes along with all the worst features of the media-dominated consumer society. Unfortunately that doesn't prove me wrong, because the modern *Zeitgeist*-machine is so all-encompassing and all-powerful that it swallows up the objectivists just as easily as it swallows up the relativists. Absolutes, certainties, foundations and authorities nowadays yo-yo in and out of fashion just as quickly as skirt-lengths and trouser-widths. So we're all in the same boat, and nobody can see the problem getting anything but worse.

But I have the advantage, because I can better tolerate transience. I freely confess that the visual beauties that mean most to me – the beauty of insects and other small animals, of birds, of the hill-country of Northern Britain, of modern painting and African tribal sculpture – all these favourite visual pleasures are modern cultural creations barely two centuries old. The same is true of moral values: when I check it out I find that nearly all of the moral causes that I care about most are cultural inventions of rather recent years. Never mind: we must love what we love, irrespective of whether any cosmic endorsement is forthcoming or not. In fact, no cosmic endorsement is to be had, and the attempts that are always made to fabricate an old pedigree for a new value are probably misguided. It would be better if we, being ephemeral ourselves, could cherish values that we know are also ephemeral, without a care. This I call 'action in the Void', when we no longer put up any demand for external support or recognition,

Many will say that 'action in the Void' is too high-flown an ideal. They still ask: 'If God is now being transformed into Culture, and if Culture is turning out to be a very capricious god – especially in the media society, and especially under capitalism – then what's to be said or done about the rapid and seemingly arbitrary shifts of fashion and values that we now witness?' One answer is the transformation of philosophy into cultural commentary by a whole variety of 'theorists' – post-modernists, post-analytic philosophers, post-structuralists and so on. Another is the parallel transformation of theology into culture-criticism, which perhaps began with Tillich, and today is practised most conspicuously by Mark C. Taylor and his allies.

Most radical of all, perhaps, are those theologies which are simply products designed to please the market, or a segment of it. Such theologies rather nakedly repackage God as green or black or whatever, but because they please so skilfully they have no difficulty in passing for orthodox.

In this book we are attempting to stick to a rather strict and traditional conception of what philosophy should do, so I am avoiding getting deflected into culture-criticism. Instead, we stay resolutely with the question: 'How can we gain eternal happiness, now we know that the values most precious to us are of recent origin and perhaps as transient and frail as we are?' We try to avoid the dissolution of philosophy into media clips and bites, and look instead to the natural and human worlds.

21. Living at the end of the world

Before Charles Darwin put forward his theory of Natural Selection, people used to claim that there was something astonishing and providential about the fact that animals and plants are so precisely adapted to their environment and way of life. Wasn't it wonderfully wise and good of God, they said, to have foreseen that with such long legs the flamingo was going to need a very long neck too, and even a bill so shaped that it could feed with its head upside-down? Look at the flamingo and praise the Lord, who hath made all things well.

But, as everyone knows, Darwin simply annihilated arguments of this type by inverting them. Where are the counter-instances? Where's the creature that is *not* adapted to its environment and way of life? Adaptation to its environment is not a surprising extra, a bonus thoughtfully added by the Creator, but the very means by which any creature comes to be here at all. Instead of seeing the animal as having been pre-designed with a view to a possible way of life, we might do better to see the constraints of its habitat and mode of life as having designed the animal. Nobody *chose* that flamingoes should look like that; they had to get to look like that in order to survive. In the way they look we can read their history.

Darwin's powerful insight depends on a switch in the way the problem of adaptation is perceived. So let us apply a similar switch to morality and the question of how we should live, and see if we get as good a result.

In most societies it has been believed that human beings should live according to Nature. There is a 'natural moral law' (as Catholics call it), or 'moral world-order' (Nietzsche's expression), which exists out there and independently of us; and we should conform our behaviour to it.

However, this traditional doctrine is obviously erroneous. Our morality is human morality and all our values are human values. The belief that we first derived our morality from an extrahuman source is as absurd as the belief that there is an eternal non-human speaker of a human language. How could there be? Because our language everywhere presupposes spatio-temporal relations, bodies, gender, emotions, sensory *qualia* (qualities) and so forth, it is as specific to us humans as our own bodies are, and clearly there cannot be any real but non-human speaker of English or Hebrew or Arabic or Sanskrit. And by the same token, our moral principles and our values everywhere presuppose our own human mode of life and social relations. So we must have invented our moralities ourselves, just as we must have invented our own languages.

Besides which, we ourselves have also obviously been the inventors of every cosmology with which we have surrounded ourselves. We painted our world-picture, so that if we recognize in it something of the values that we live by, the reason is simply that we put them there.

These considerations bring about the 180° turn: we don't derive our values from Nature; Nature has derived her values from us.

Consider, for example, successive images of Nature in Britain. In the mid-eighteenth century of the squirearchy and the Argument from Design, the ideological emphasis was upon harmony, stability and the wisdom of the established order of things. Nature was perceived as a calm, wise and kindly Mother. In the mid-nineteenth-century of industrialism and free trade, the ideological emphasis was upon competition and progress through struggle. Nature seemed cruel: for our own eventual good she has imposed a very harsh market discipline upon us and upon all other creatures. But in the mid-twentieth century Nature changed again. Pure brutal economic individualism of the sort traditionally favoured by Anglo-Saxon millionaires began to look destructive. There was a rapid growth of ecological and ethological studies in the life sciences, and of popular environmentalism. Nature began to be portrayed as an abused Woman, as in Sally McFague's book, *The Body of God* (SCM Press and Minneapolis: Fortress Press 1993). Nature was a beautiful, balanced ecosystem, but Man has ill-treated and damaged her. Healing and restoring her will be difficult and costly, but it must be done.

In the past people used to say that we should live according to Nature: now we see that Nature lives according to humanity. It is idle to pretend to derive our values from her, now that we see how she gets all her perceived values from us.

As we follow up this insight, we begin to understand that we painted all the scenery, the backdrop against which we live our lives. Which means that, morally speaking, we really have come of age. We stand alone. We are the only legislators. Our moral preferences are radically our own, without any extrinsic or independent support or subsequent ratification at all. Our valuations are only as strong as our own belief in them and commitment to them.

Just how novel and startling is the position just stated? Many people will want to point out that something like it has a long history in our tradition, beginning with the farewell charges of Moses and Joshua in the Hebrew Bible. The prophetic voice warns that we have come to a turning point and must make, 'this day', 'Now', the decision that will be determinative of our entire future. Something similar is said by Jesus, in the context of his belief in the early arrival of the *Parousia* – the end of history and the coming of the Reign of God on earth. It seems to imply a thoroughgoing voluntarism: as in theology it was said that God creates the world by a *fiat* of his Will, so the individual under God was called upon likewise to create his or her own future by a once-and-for-all *fiat* of the will.

In later religious practice the taking of life vows, in marriage or to the religious life, had a somewhat similar weight and force, so that the notion that human beings can and must create reality by decision of the will is not just a modern aberration (as many seem to think) but has long been established in the West. It was made prominent in philosophy by Kant through the idea of the primacy of practical reason, and was then popularized by the motley crew of philosophers, from Kierkegaard to Sartre, who used to be called 'existentialists'.

However, most of these thinkers and teachers called upon the individual to be strong and to make a fresh start at some particular moment of crisis. Israel entering the promised Land is called upon to decide whom she will serve; Jesus' hearer is called upon to repent because today is the day before the Day of Judgment; Kierkegaard warns that the modern age is an age of culture, of world-historical development and of massification in which 'the individual', as a category, may be lost. Heidegger and Sartre write against the background of the perceived moral vacuum left by the First and Second World Wars respectively. The institutions which used to be perceived as embodying and as sustaining the moral order are now destroyed or discredited, and it's up to courageous individuals to create new values and build new and better institutions.

These prophetic and existentialist calls to decision were, then, issued against the background of a sense of social or even cosmic breakdown. What I have been describing has been a little different, and is as close to the young Hegelians as it is to Kierkegaard. I'm saying that our knowledge has grown and grown, and with it the habit of critical thinking has grown, until we have become more completely demythologized than (until very recently) anybody would have thought possible. I do believe that a few of us are getting to be more demythologized even than Nietzsche himself. Human knowledge has grown until we can't help recognizing that it is after all only our knowledge, only our world, only our morality, only our religion, only our rationality, our philosophy, our language . . . and after this 'anthropomonism' (*Only Human*, 1985) the next step is that we ourselves also are demythologized away, leaving only the flux of sign-formed events (*The Time Being*, 1992), and therefore an extremely lightweight world in which the self itself is only a transient 'literary' effect, somewhat as a *dramatis persona* is only a transient effect produced by the performance of a drama.

The old Western self, as described by Augustine and Descartes, stood back a little from the empirical world, to inhabit the private sub-world of its own thoughts and its own self-consciousness before God. But now a double reduction has occurred: it has simultaneously brought us down into, and made us only a part of, the flux of the world; and at the same time it has wonderfully given the world to us. The new order is an improvement: it is better to be a human being rather than to be an angel in a house of clay.

In any case, that is how things now are. Jesus and the existentialists spoke at times of one-off historical crisis, and summoned an élite corps of volunteers to step forward and deal with it. I'm describing something a little different, a permanent and general cultural condition that we are all now entering, the logical outcome of the way things have been going for a long time – since Descartes, or even perhaps a bit earlier. Many people already feel that this is how it is; and their number will steadily increase.

In summary, we are here talking, not of a one-off crisis which demands a special response from a few heroic individuals, but of a permanent cultural condition which demands a general adjust-ment on everybody's part. The world itself, our values, and we ourselves are looking very much lighter, more transient and thinner than formerly, and there is no longer any eternal or external support or background. I am, remember, not saying that we are alone, lost and homeless in the universe, in the young Heidegger's sense. On the contrary, I have emphasized as strongly as may be that the Universe is very homely indeed. We made the only picture of the universe that we have, so naturally we made it 'anthropic', as some unphilosophical physicists are nowadays putting it. We gave to Nature her marvellous beauty and her human values. We recognize in the world about us an expressive objectification of ourselves, the concrete universal human. The world about us is our own work of art and our chief consolation.

But we are alone in it. We have become like artists who must live for, by and in our work. So what I mean by 'living at the end of the world' is: coming to a full realization of what has happened, and rising to the challenge of a much more art-centred vision of life. It is a change that takes a lot of getting accustomed to.

The changeover from absolute monarchy to democracy is perhaps the first and clearest image of what's happened. Under absolute monarchy everything has a rank, a place on a scale that runs up to what is eternal and absolute. Everything gets legitimated, has its value fixed, from above. By relating yourself to the Absolute, you are assured of your own given reality, your given value and your given place in the whole scheme of things. Your standing may be only middling or indeed very low, but at least you know where and what you are. Which is quite something, because in democracy nothing is fixed or absolute, and everything is relative and mobile. All meanings, truths and values are produced by a fluid and shifting human consensus that never gets finalized.

Another way of showing what has happened will describe how the sign has changed from symbol to signal. In premodern times the most potent, world-building and society-changing communicative action was ritual. The signs used in religious rituals were very condensed, heavy and authoritative. Through them we related ourselves to the eternal order. But for today's equivalent we should watch men gesticulating and signalling to each other on a trading-floor or a flight-deck, at an auction, a racecourse, a playing-field, a market or an exchange. By the signalling information is passed, and bargains are struck. Any ambiguity might be dangerous or might give rise to costly disputes, so the sign has to be very simple and univocal like a road-sign, or like the signs on the controls of a machine.

So we changed from symbol to signal, and from a ritual world to a world that is like a communications-network or a market. It's a very noisy and crowded market: the cultural resources that we can tap into just in our own towns, and even in our own houses, give us ready access to other places, other times, and all of human knowledge. And many commentators do not at all like this abundance: indeed many of the leading theorists of postmodern culture, such as Jean Baudrillard, are romantic conservatives and blackly pessimistic about the way things are developing.

Such pessimism needs a reply. Here it is: a very long tradition in our culture always said that at the End of all Things everything becomes either simply human or at least, completely as we would wish it to be. Everything is either ourselves or just as we want it.

Such a state of things has, in slightly different ways, been the implied goal of religion, of critical thinking, of science and technology, and even of politics.

In *religion*, Heaven, Paradise, the City of God and the Kingdom of God are all symbols of a world fully humanized, reconciled and perfected. As for *critical thinking*, it exactly reverses – always *has* reversed – mythical thinking. Mythical thinking projects outwards, objectifying, persuading us to see Culture as Nature and human images and conventions as entrenched features of objective Reality; whereas critical thinking works in the opposite direction, turning Nature back into Culture again, as we come to see that what was sold to us as objective and unalterable natural law is after all just a human product. Thus, in every sphere, critical thinking demythologizes by resolving so-called 'objective Reality' back into its human basis. The logical conclusion of critical thinking is thoroughgoing humanistic non-realism, as everything, but everything, gets brought down into the flux of human communication.

As for *science*, by seeking a complete fundamental science of nature and a complete description of the natural world, it too seeks the complete en-culturalization and human appropriation of Nature. *Technology* likewise seeks complete control of nature, to such an extent that there will no longer be any clear distinction between the world of brute and obdurate fact and the world of our dreams. In so far as realism rests upon such a distinction, technology too aims at non-realism. Finally, our *politics* too is orientated towards radical humanism, in so far as liberal democracy is the End of politics, and in liberal democracy we come to see that all meanings, truth, values and even Reality itself are but the products of our own changing, evolving conversational consensus.

Thus a world radically humanized, a world reconciled and transparent to us, a world that answers to our hearts' desire, is the common goal of religion, critical thinking, scientific theory, technology and politics in the Western tradition. And such a world has increasingly come into view since the 1960s, as we see religion at last being thoroughly demythologized into Left religious humanism, critical thinking moving into antirealism, scientific theory becoming more complete than ever, technology globalizing all processes of exchange, and liberal democratic politics no longer having any intellectually-serious rival.

This is not in any way to conceal or deny the dreadful evils that today threaten all and are overwhelming some people. My purpose is rather different: since people first became aware of large-scale historical and cultural change it has become common for philosophers to propose that we should live not by tradition, but by a vision of the world that is coming-to-be. A humanistic philosophy of the future is in one way or another proposed by Hegel, Marx, Feuerbach, Nietzsche and many others; and the 'non-realistic cosmic humanism' of this present essay may be seen as indebted to that tradition. Instead of deriving our world-view and our ethic from an unchanging tradition that demands our obedience, we derive them from an art-vision of what is coming to be, the way things might be, could be, will be. (In theological language, that is eschatological living.) Hence the earlier suggestion that a philosophy may be seen as a network of metaphors that help us to view the world as a fit arena for the living of a certain kind of life (pp.9f., above) I have tried to follow my own maxim, by asking: 'How may the world be viewed as a place in which human beings may find fulfilment and eternal happiness?'

And although I undertook to eschew theology, something of it has crept in after all.

Note

Here I should confess that a considerable ethical change has taken place. A decade or so ago I commended an ethic that was protestant, combative and strenuous. The believer 'cannot help but be in some measure inwardly alienated, for he lives by another value scale. He is a critic and protester, who has here no continuing city.' And so on, and indeed on: the believer was differentiated from his neighbours not by holding supernatural beliefs, but by standing at a slight angle to life. Later, he is to be found energetically battling to create new values.

Now, as death gets closer, one becomes 'easy, going'. The world becomes more and more beautiful, and the mood more quietistic. One must still act, because one must go out into expression in order to find redemption. But the old metaphoric of restlessness and combat – 'fighting' for causes, and so on – is now replaced by an ethic of world-love and acceptance.

So I here repent of my former self-conscious strenuousness.

22. Summary

What is there?

1. (to be read aloud) There is at least *language*. Here we are in it; and in any case, the existence of language cannot coherently be denied, denial being itself a linguistic act.

    For there to be language, moving as these sentences now are in being produced and received, there must also be temporality and a discharge and scattering of energies.

2. There must be *temporality*, in the sense of unidirectional succession in the production, presentation and scanning of a chain of signs. (There need not necessarily be 'linear time' in any stronger sense, for cyclical time also may be unidirectional.)

3. There must be *scattering energies*, because uttered language needs a material 'body' to ride upon or to modulate. Language is *broadcast*, or *published*.

4. There is at least, then, an outpouring and scattering stream of language-formed events. And we do best to picture the world at large as *a beginningless, endless and outsideless stream of language-formed events* that continually pours forth and passes away. The stream of events becomes real and determinate, or 'formed', in being read as language by us.

5. By being read, in one language or another (natural, mathematical etc.), the elements of the world become experience, and by being described they become public, or 'real'. Thus the real world is the public world, which is the-world-in-language, *our* world.

6. Our worst mistake is that of supposing the world of consciousness to be a private subworld within each person. No: the world of consciousness is simply the public world, the world that our language has fixed, objectified, illuminated and made public. Our consciousness is simply our participation in this common world.

7. A chain of signs like this one can claim to be an epitome of everything in so far as (*a*), it states that the world itself consists of lots and lots more stuff like this; and (*b*), the signs it contains resonate with and evoke many, many other strands in the flux of world-events.

8. Thus philosophy must (*a*), represent the world as a many-stranded stream of events-read-as-signs; and (*b*), must work somewhat as poetry does, by employing highly-condensed and evocative metaphors.

9. Human life is radically linguistic, because it is language that gives to the stream of events, not only the flowing continuity, but also the *identifiable aims*, that our life requires. (To live a human life, I must not only have desires, but know what they are. Or at least what some of them are. I must have goals, and I need to be able to make up narrative accounts of how I may achieve my goals.)

10. In practical philosophy the world is seen under totalizing metaphors that enable us to view it as a fit arena for the successful pursuit of a certain way of life.

11. All readings of the stream of events are highly selective-and-constructive.

12. When the stream of events is read from a first-person-singular standpoint, and in a vocabulary that gives priority to one's own interests and desires, then it is seen as the world of experience or *subjectivity*. (But still, my world is simply my angle upon the common world.)

13. When the stream of events is read from a third-person standpoint, then it is seen as the *objective* world – as, for example, the world of our physical-object language, or the world of some form of scientific theory.

14. In the objective world we recognize other persons, with angles upon the world other than our own. Thus the second-person standpoint, and with it the possibility of ethical and political thought and action, arises as a synthesis of the first-person and the third-person readings of the world.

15. This synthesis is *love*.

16. Everything is made of only one sort of stuff, namely the stream of language-formed events, and the very same bits of world-stuff may be taken up into various constructions – for example, into both your subjectivity and mine. Selfhoods overlap, it may be very considerably.

17. The happiness that comes when one realizes that one is completely immersed in and interwoven with the whole endless flux of things is *ecstatic immanence*.

18. As a living being, one is an organism composed of various organs or subsystems which have slightly different aims. (There is, for example, a potential discordance between the need to preserve one's own life and the need, at whatever cost, to pass on one's genes.) Thus there is – it seems, irremediably – some conflict of forces within the self, which shows up in every first-person account of things as the distinction between text and subtext, conscious and subconscious etc. This conflict is *ambivalence*. 'Mixed feelings.'

19. Ambivalence within the self is at least partly resolved and relieved by talking, by artistic expression and by theorizing the world.

20. The sign as such is a compromise-formation, and all our symbolic expressions are more unified and beautiful than we who have originated them.

21. As our productive and expressive life-activity is a continual *creation* of the world of experience, so too the happiness that comes when we see our conflicting aims and feelings resolved in the beauty of the world is *our objective redemption*, that is, our redemption achieved in and through our expression. Hence 'expressionism'.

22. When we see in the public world our own objective redemption, we see the world as being *ours* in the strongest sense; that is, we see in it the concrete universal human, reconciled and perfected. (This 'cosmic humanism' is possible because (*a*), we make the world look the way it does to us; and (*b*), the world is made of just the same stuff as the self is made of.)

23. Because there is no subjective immortality, we can be happy in recognizing in the continuance of the world our own objective immortality; and because there is no subjective redemption, we can be happy in recognizing in the beauty of the world our own objective redemption.

24. The way to this eternal happiness is by the love (12 – 15 above) which enables us to escape from a purely first-personal or subjective view of our condition.

Note

This short formal summary was written for and presented to a meeting of the Cambridge 'D' Society. A distinguished philosopher snorted 'Idealism' (or perhaps *meant* a snort, even if he didn't quite snort audibly). However, what I have presented is not pure linguistic idealism. Rather as Derrida nowadays says that language has an Other which he calls 'force', so I have pictured language's Other as the outpouring flux of world-energies that it needs to provide it with its 'body'. However, language does not 'exist' apart from its body, and we have no extra-linguistic access to that body.

In any case, having stated my system, I ought to cross it out, lest I be thought to have relapsed into an obsolete kind of metaphysics. For on my own premisses our thinking is constrained by the forms of representation available to it; that is, by our language. So what *can* I pretend to add to what is already given to us all with and within the resources of our beautiful language? Put it shortly: good writing says everything already, so what more *can* be said? How can a philosophy text get to say anything that is not said equally well in a poem?

In this present text, in talking about *consciousness* I am not able (and nobody ever will be able) to go beyond the metaphors of light, brightness, clarity that every English speaker already has; and in talking about our feeling for *life*, I can't go beyond the familiar metaphors of enjoyment, relish, appetite and zest that everyone already has in their vocabulary. If we truly know and love our language, we know it all.

So, although my small summary is quite intricately composed it needs to be crossed out or put in scare quotes, lest I give the impresson that I am claiming more than anyone can or should claim.

In response to questions and criticisms, I should add that a number of points in the Summary were explained in detail in *After All* or in earlier writings, and have not been repeated in the present book.

In addition to *witness* and *tell*, another verb neatly illustrates the way language and reality are interwoven, namely *describe*. On 3 June 1994, happy, I walked with my companion on the moors above Farndale. Over our heads a curlew described neat circles and gave off warning cries, by way of pin-pointing our position and alerting the whole district to our presence. Acts of description don't just replicate the world in language: they draw lines, separate, mark out, single out, highlight and advise. Descriptions structure the world in a way relevant to the fulfilment of some purpose or other – raising young curlews, for example.

Appendix: Theology in the here and now

An ancient myth found all over the Old World relates that in the beginning human beings and the gods lived together on earth. The gods were just like us humans, but a notch or two bigger, more beautiful and more powerful, and so blue-blooded that in India they are remembered to this day as being blue-skinned, all over. That did not make them unattractive to our women. Far from it, because quite apart from the business of Krishna and all those cowgirls, both the Hebrew Bible (Gen. 6. 2–4) and the Greeks have preserved traditions of extensive crossbreeding, the offspring of which included giants, Titans and Titanesses, demigods, heroes and sacred kings. This reveals the very interesting fact that in the days when the gods were closest to us humans they were thought of – and in the most convincing manner proved themselves actually to *be* – members of the same biological species. The only difference was that while the gods were immortal (and often blue), humans were mortal and the hybrid beings were mostly males, large, powerful and unusually long-lived. Biologists call this 'hybrid vigour'.

It is very noticeable that the gods were not in the least abashed by their own sexual irregularities, but continued graciously handing out advice and admonitions to us humans. In this respect they resembled our royalty rather than our politicians: there was a tacit understanding that one was expected to emulate them in some ways and not others. In their personal behaviour they were a law unto themselves and did exactly as they pleased, but when they were consciously setting the fashion and giving an example to us mortals, then their way of doing something was the right way, and would be so forever.

Those were the good days; that was the Age of Gold. But somehow a chill developed in the relations between humans and gods, and the gods began to withdraw, at first to the upper slopes of the Holy Mountain, and then to Heaven. Some say that we had offended them by our sinfulness. But however that may be, the departure of the gods was gradual. For a while they would occasionally reappear on earth in person, and then for a further period they spoke to us through the mouths of oracles and prophets. But eventually appearances and voices ceased altogether.

During the period of gradual withdrawal two distinct religious systems overlapped, and it was possible one day to be offering sacrifices as if the gods were now far off up in Heaven, and then only a short while later to find yourself actually talking to the same god in person. Both Homer and the book of *Genesis* describe such a mixed period. But as the gods withdrew finally, their role in superintending us was taken over by the apparatus of organized religion. This means principally 'hierarchy', which is technically government by a college of priests. The priests control the cult, including the sacrificial system and the annual cycle of festivals, and they administer religious law. In due course the priests also came to control the scriptures and the standards of right belief.

This system – hierarchy and the apparatus of mediated religion – does three jobs. First, the priests are like bailiffs or stewards, responsible for managing the gods' estates during the time of their absence. Secondly, the priests are also responsible for maintaining and controlling the approved channels of communication between humans and gods. And thirdly, the disciplinary apparatus of mediated religion is so effective that it makes civilization possible. It teaches the people memory, patience and hope. They are to cherish their communal past, to think long-term, and to live peacefully under the sacred Law that the gods delivered to us upon the Holy Mountain before they finally left.

Thus it was the withdrawal of the gods which led to the first creation of the disciplinary instruments that have fitted people for historical, civilized life. The historical human being lives under the Law, in a state of sin, and waiting for redemption. But a disciplinary civilization can't help but also remind people that it is only a second best. It inevitably encourages nostalgia for the lost innocence and happiness of Paradise, and what Mircea Eliade has called 'the desire to be always, effortlessly, at the heart of the world of reality, of the sacred' (*Patterns in Comparative Religion*, Sheed & Ward 1958, § 146).

How are human beings to get back to the old longed-for divine heart and centre of things? To some extent they can achieve it by ritual, as when they go on pilgrimage to a holy place such as Rome, Jerusalem or Mecca, that they see as being the Centre of the world. Indeed, such is the curious character of religious thought that there are many Centres, including the holy mountain, the axis of the world, the Cathedral, the local parish church and even the roof-tree of one's own house. Symbolic ways of thinking are very hospitable, and there is also a seasonal Centre, for people believe that through the annual cycle of feasts, and especially at Christmas, they are returning again and again into their own lost Origin.

Underlying all this, the strongest hope of all is the hope that the gods will one day come back to earth, and resume control from the priests and kings who have been managing their affairs in their absence. People hope for a return of the old innocent intimacy. They even hope that God will be born of a woman, born in our hearts, and establish his permanent residence within and amongst us. This is called the Kingship or Reign of God, much hoped-for in the Bible and always associated with talk of the heart or spirit. The language used for the return of the divine into the human is remarkably strong, so strong that religious believers themselves can't see how strong it is. It's a language of union and of reciprocal indwelling, we in God's heart and he in ours, his spirit and ours conjoined and concentric. This confusion of God and humans is sometimes called by theologians 'deification'. It may seem remarkable, but I hinted earlier that in the beginning gods and humans were more-or-less of the same species anyway.

Since God *is* spirit, his Spirit is his very self, his essence, presence and power, and even his own knowledge of himself. So that when God's very own Spirit is poured out like water into human hearts, there to speak in and with our spirit and to inspire the living of a new and supernatural form of life, the divine is no longer alienated from the human. They *flow* together like two liquids mingling, as is in one way and another so often said in the metaphors of religion. They amalgamate. Brahman and the Atman, God and the soul, the core of the human self and the ground of the Universe, the Lover and the Beloved, simply coincide. They become One, and there is no longer a separate God. The language really is as strong as that. Reciprocal indwelling, for example, with God in my heart and me in his, is a geometrical feat imaginable only if we become concentric and identical. The later development of doctrine, which chose to literalize some metaphors and not others, rather conspicuously chose not to literalize this one, because it implies the Death of God.

In later Christian language, therefore, only God's *Grace* was like a liquid injected into us, and not God's own *Spirit*. The Spirit is usually spoken of as a *light*, shed in our hearts and illuminating our minds. This avoids the suggestion of commingling. But the early Kingdom-hope was nevertheless a hope that religious alienation would soon come to an end. God would return into the human heart, human beings would be liberated, and the oppressive discipline of organized religion would disappear because it was no longer needed. As the Rabbis said, if all Israel were to keep the Law fully for one day, the Kingdom would come – meaning, that the Law is not an end in itself. When we can fully keep the Law, we'll no longer need the Law and it can fall away. A man whose broken leg is mended hardly notices himself dropping his crutches and his stick. So the external supportive apparatus would not be required. The elaborate cult would go, leaving only 'the sacrifice of praise and thanksgiving' (*sacrificium laudis*, the Eucharist). In the Kingdom of God there would be no objective God, only the god in one's heart, the subjective experience of one's own recovered divinity.

All this was briefly glimpsed as coming to pass in the New Testament period. Jesus of Nazareth preached that the long historical period of waiting was over. The divine was coming back into the human realm, and organized religion – especially, Temple religion – was coming to an end. It is because Jesus is such bad news for organized religion that he appears in the Temple or at the synagogue only to cause trouble, every single time. One simply cannot imagine him sitting quiet and docile in the midst of a congregation. Every time he appears, he starts an argument. But he does not plan to be King in the Kingdom of God himself, nor does he speak of God as becoming an objectively and visibly reigning Monarch on earth; for the god of Jesus lives in the human heart and is known only in secret. Returning to reign on earth, God takes up his throne in the human heart; *hidden*. The divine is no longer objectified in a great disciplinary institution, but instead becomes dispersed into human subjectivity. God thus dies in order to set us free: or, to put it another way, Jesus' view of what God will show himself to be is *non-realist*.

Now we see a whole cluster of ideas beginning to click together in the early Christian period. The first idea is the idea of history as the schooldays of the human race, the disciplinary period, dominated by the power-structures of the 'organized' type of religion that lasts from the withdrawal of the gods until their return. Historical time is thus linear eschatological time, the time of waiting under discipline for Redemption, and the End of History is the same event as the coming of the Kingdom of God and the Death of God. When God is absent, he seems to be an objective being who lives in Heaven. So God is real while he is remote, in another world. But when God is present he is not an objective being but only freedom, the power of life and of the Word in one's own subjectivity. God is objectified only in his absence. When present, he is just people's own charisma, their creativity, their freedom.

So the End of History, the coming of the Kingdom of God, the Death of God, the outpouring of God's spirit in human hearts, and the final liberation of humanity are ideas all interlinked and briefly glimpsed in the first forty years or so of Christian history. Jesus understands them, and they can still be read in Paul; but then they were lost, and it is not easy to say why.

Here, briefly, is an hypothesis to explain what may have happened: in the first half-century the infant Church was not clearly distinguished from the Synagogue. When Jerusalem fell in AD 70 and the Temple was destroyed, the shock to the Jewish Diaspora was profound. Not surprisingly, Juda*ism* set about creating itself by codifying itself as a new Book-centred (rather than place-centred) religious system, governed by occasional Councils or Synods of Rabbis, meeting as need arose. This obliged the Universal Church similarly to create itself, codifying and defining itself as a new religious system distinct from Judaism. Thus the destruction of the Temple, instead of being interpreted as confirmation of Jesus' original message, became instead the starting-point for the creation of two new religions, codified autonomous synagogue-Judaism, and the Catholic Church. In the first generation or two God was fully dispersed into human lives, human bodies, so that each individual believer's own body was a Temple, and there was no objectified God. But now first the whole organized Church community (Eph. 2; I Peter 2), and then increasingly *the objectified Church-system*, began to be called a new Temple. The Catholic and Apostolic Church, with its powerful hierarchy, its sacraments, its Law and its religion of divine *absence* thus became a thundering reinstatement of exactly the mediated institutional type of religion that Jesus had said was coming to an end. Jesus prophesied the destruction of the Temple, but the Church rebuilt Temple-religion on a much larger scale in his name.

Christianity's resulting self-falsification is absurd, but we take it for granted. In a way we know that Jesus and his followers were a group of lay people who had no institutional standing or authority, but at the same time we are somehow persuaded to accept the received idea that Jesus is a King and a cosmic High Priest, that he more-or-less appointed Peter to be Pope and the other disciples to be Apostles and (later) Bishops, and that Jesus therefore personally founded the Church, commissioned the Sacred Ministry, and instituted the Sacraments. Carrying on the good work, the Apostles between them compiled the Creed and wrote the New Testament. Thus the entire system of the One Holy Catholic and Apostolic Church was all established by the very first generation.

This remarkable transfiguration of Jesus and his untidy band of New Age travellers in effect squeezed out their original Kingdom-religion, and it was forgotten. Jesus' own message played almost no part in Catholic Christianity, which through various historical upheavals and schisms ran its course until the year 1500 or so. Then with the arrival of the modern age there began a long series of attempts to re-discover an original Christian message prior to the development of Catholic Christianity.

It has proved extraordinarily difficult. The New Testament text is already rather highly edited, and in addition our reading of what has reached us is so very constrained by tradition, by power-interests and by old pschological demands and habits. If you doubt this, try asking people to name Jesus' four brothers. They are listed twice in the Gospels, but for all sorts of traditional and psychological reasons we simply don't want to know about Jesus' brothers. We just cannot bear the thought that younger siblings edged him out of first place in his Mother's affections. So we all of us forget their names; and a similar partial blindness and amnesia affects the whole of the rest of our reading of the New Testament.

The truth is that we read badly because we are so scarred by Church history. But the struggle for a new post-ecclesiastical Kingdom-theology has been going on irregularly since the Reformation. Thomas Munzer himself was already looking for something of the sort. The Quakers and others of the Reformation Left sought to bring spiritual Power down from Heaven and disperse it into human hearts. Muggleton, Reeve and others in the Commonwealth period declared that all Three Persons of the Trinity had been incarnate in Jesus Christ and in him had died. The Swedenborgians and Blake thought of Jesus Christ as 'the only God', meaning that a new 'divine humanism' must replace the old pyramid of Powers above us. Both Kant and Hegel set out to demythologize God, Kant making God into the guiding moral Ideal that is immanent in our Reason, and Hegel making God into *Geist*, Spirit or Mind, our historically evolving communal consciousness – perhaps (you might say) our culture. And then amongst the Young Hegelians the transformation of orthodox theology into religious humanism was completed by the 1840s, and reached even benighted Britain in the same decade.

In these movements we see a new religious outlook struggling to be born. Because our old language is breaking down, and a new vocabulary has not yet become established, there is no single name for this post-ecclesiastical or post-Catholic religion. I have used several. Thinking of the Quakers, I have on occasion called it *a dispersed, Pentecost-Christianity*. Thinking of the great nineteenth-century figures, I have called it *Christian humanism*. Thinking of Nietzsche's phrase, 'active nihilism', I have called it *active non-realism*. Recently, I have used the phrase *post-Christianity*. Others call it simply *Christian atheism*, and here by calling it *Kingdom-theology* I am reminding myself of the work of Johannes Weiss and Albert Schweitzer.

In 1893 Weiss published a short book called *Jesus' Proclamation of the Kingdom of God*. His thesis, later taken up by Albert Schweitzer, was that Jesus' whole message had revolved around one topic only, the imminent end of history and the arrival of the Kingdom of God. Schweitzer adds the very important idea that in the first generation or two people were trying to realize the Kingdom by anticipation, seizing in advance the features and the powers of the Kingdom-world, bit-by-bit. Weiss and Schweitzer between them have persuaded many or most theologians that the original Jesus was not a bit like the Divine Christ of the Church. He was a purely Jewish figure, a prophet of the Kingdom of God. He hoped he would be vindicated, but when he was arraigned, condemned and martyred for his 'blasphemy' against the Temple he died in despair, abandoned by God.

There has been something astonishing and richly ironical about the insouciance with which the orthodox Christian establishment has received all this. It is as if they were quietly saying to themselves: 'Well, we never thought all that much of the man Jesus, anyway. Especially, we didn't much care for his attacks on people like us. So it's actually rather good news that the human Jesus did not *know* he was God Incarnate, and came to a sticky end. But as Jesus is proved wrong, God is proved right! In and through the life and death of Jesus, God was at work establishing a new and eternal Covenant, a way to salvation for the whole human race. And he has chosen us to manage it all for him.' Thus the orthodox Church establishment greets Schweitzer's picture of Jesus as a pre-Christian figure, a failed Jewish prophet, with a certain satisfaction. It not only gratifies their residual antisemitism, it also proves that Kingdom-religion is not yet a viable option anyway. Humankind were not ready for it then, and still aren't now. So they conclude, with the Grand Inquisitor, that Church-religion is still the best available compromise between Kingdom-religion and the facts of life.

I am suggesting, however, that the way things are going in the modern and post-modern periods indicates that people *are* now ready for Kingdom-religion. For consider its main features: the Kingdom-world is a world with no Beyond. People no longer need to look to another and better world after this life, and they no longer believe in progress. Rather, it is a time when people live in and for the present. They are content with, and reconciled to, the world about them. For them, *this* world is the real world.

Accordingly, the Kingdom-world is a world in which people no longer *look up*. They simply don't see those above them as their betters. They have outgrown *both* deference *and* deferral. They don't want to spend their lives within disciplinary institutions that promise pie in the sky and jam tomorrow. They are radically democratic. They have grown up, and they want it now. They want to see human fulfilment and human happiness in this world.

Thirdly, the Kingdom world is a world in which people are no longer content to live permanently alienated from their own bodies, from Nature, and from God. In a word, modern human beings are no longer willing to be foreigners in their own world, and no longer willing to live in a state of servitude.

People are at last growing up. So what will their religion be like? Their God will be radically immanent and their philosophy expressionist. They will feel life as a stream of energies fountaining up within the self, becoming shaped by language, and flowing out to form and reform the world of experience. They thus experience, day by day, the divine life coursing through them, and the creation of their world happening in and through their own activity. Such human beings live like gods. Objectified and absent, the old God was in effect Tradition deified. All creativity was abstracted from people and concentrated in him. He had fixed everything, and you simply fitted yourself into the order that he had established. But now when God returns into human hearts, people get their own creativity back again. A religion of creativity replaces the old religion of obedience.

The older ecclesiastical type of religion worked first by splitting the world and the self, and then by offering channels of Grace and healing that would slowly join everything up again. So the divine was separated from the human, heaven from earth, reason from sensuousness, the long-term from the short-term, and the soul from the body. By thus splitting up everything, the ideology set us all longing for healing and redemption. The Church's faith and her channels of Grace were then offered to heal all the wounds; and they really did work. You were indeed on the way to full healing and salvation. But you would not see everything fully restored this side of the grave. You must spend your whole life under discipline, on the Way, and in a state of subjection to the authority of the Church (and the king).

It was a great system, designed to last forever because it postponed forever the salvation that it made you long for and led you towards. What is short-circuiting it today is the fact that modern human beings who live after Darwin, do not accept the dualism upon which it is all predicated. We can now do better than that.

When I say that we now need to spell out and to start living a Kingdom-religion people protest by bringing up the problem of evil. But in reply we can say that the doctrines of metaphysical evil and Original Sin, and the disciplinary apparatus that they are used to justify, combine to make things a lot worse than they need be. Indeed, I argue that when the self is melted down completely into the world, and the world is at the same time completely given to us, in the ways I have described, the outcome is unexpectedly blissful. Despite the persistence of conflict and suffering, I speak of the Kingdom as having come.

To say this – that the Kingdom has come – is doubtless to invite misunderstanding. People will hear me as having said something fatuously optimistic, and perhaps as claiming that a supernatural event has taken place. But that is not at all what I am saying. Rather, I am saying that we live after the death of God and the end of metaphysical realism: we live in the American century, the century of 'the plain style' and 'the common man'. In our time we all of us know in our hearts that there is no reality greater or more primal than the world of ordinary language and everyday life; there is no other world, no higher or more privileged point of view and nothing better yet to come. Where we are is the centre of the world and the place of creation. Ordinariness is ultimate and outsideless; that is it, and there is no Beyond.

To say that the Kingdom has come, then, is simply to say that we now recognize that everydayness is all there is. We need to give up the idea that our life waits to be given meaning from somewhere external to it. There is no man with a big hat, no expert, no celebrity who is more closely in touch with the heart and centre of things than we are already.

Thus a Kingdom-theology does not pretend to give us good news about external sources of support and help. Instead it seeks to return us to ourselves and to everyday life, in such a way that we are no longer fretful. Instead, we are content.

To indicate what Kingdom-religion might be like, let me end by retelling a well-known story about Henri Matisse. Asked whether he believed in God, the old man replied, 'Yes, when I'm working'. Looking at his work, one knows what he meant. Piety, not as patient submission and devotion, but as the production of joy.

Note

The first major thinker to attempt to move from ecclesiastical theology to kingdom theology was Kant. An interesting and persuasive account of the rise of Christianity from a kingdom-theology viewpoint is Thomas Sheehan's *The First Coming: How the Kingdom of God became Christianity* (Random House 1986). T. J. J. Altizer, in for example *The Genesis of God* (Louisville, Kentucky: John Knox/Westminster Press 1993), sees the realization of the Kingdom of God as God's passing into complete immanence – that is, dying – and thereby bringing about our resurrection. This seems to equate the Resurrection with our coming at last fully to ourselves in the here and now. Extraordinary.

Prosopography

Philosophers are not scholars. Scholars are disciplined characters who study texts and are much exercised about questions of objectivity, accuracy and doing justice. Their job is to establish a correct text, to place it in relation to other texts, to interpret it justly and so on. But philosophers are quite different. Like artists, they have to invent everything they produce. They must try to go back to the very beginning. Or, if they are seriously up-to-date, they worry about how you can ever *begin* to say that the whole idea of beginning at the very beginning was a complete mistake, anyway.

However that may be, philosophers have to be unscholarly. They are neither joiners nor disciples: they can neither simply adopt and share the beliefs of a group nor simply be faithful interpreters of someone else's ideas. Philosophers must try to find out and be true to what they themselves think. Strange, that what they produce has some hope of being true and interesting only if it is the purest fiction.

There is more than one way of doing this. Wittgenstein used to boast of how little of the great philosophers of the past he had actually read, and would sometimes decline to attend a lecture because when working he 'didn't want to take in any foreign goods'. You could say – to put it picturesquely – that other people's ideas just didn't fit comfortably into his head. They scratched his mind, and made him irritable. (Even more irritable than usual).

Others, however, find irritation very helpful. Some feminists have read Freud precisely in order to be enraged by him and thereby be stimulated to work out their own ideas in opposition to his. Freud is, after all, better than anyone at giving feminists a good idea of what it is they are up against.

Another form of 'strong misreading' has been used by Deleuze: the ways in which I find myself obstinately misreading writers from the tradition help me to discover where I myself am trying to go.

– Which is the explanation for this prosopography. Although I set out hoping to write democratic philosophy, with the idea that if philosophy can no longer be democratized then it is dead and should be abandoned as a subject, a certain amount of academic name-dropping seems to have happened nevertheless. Why have all these names crept into the text? As readers of P. G. Wodehouse will know, in the English-speaking world only Jeeves reads philosophy, and even he seems to stop at Spinoza. Nietzsche, we gather, is regarded as 'quite radically unsound, Sir'. Nowadays, when there are so few Jeeveses left to write for, the classic names from the past should surely be left out?

Nevertheless, I have not cut them out. They stand – as clues to a private mythology. Rather as in cinema a brief shot of the Eiffel Tower is a way of saying that the action has moved to Paris, so the mention of a name like that of Schopenhauer is shorthand for a certain literary personality, mood, style of argument, way of thinking, 'position'. A prosopography is strictly a list or directory of persons real or imaginary, with brief details about them, and this one may perhaps serve both as an index of names, and as a key to the writer's personal canon. These names signify bodies of writing and literary personalities that have become interwoven with the way words run in me.

It seems that one's canon changes as the years go by. Recent events have evidently tilted me even more towards thorough-going naturalism, towards biology and towards philosophies that see reality as produced by perpetually-conflicting forces. I start wanting to read Davidson on language, rather than Derrida. I pick up James, Bergson, Deleuze. Heidegger hovers reproachfully. Death gets ever more attractive and interesting, and I turn to Heraclitus, Nietzsche, Bataille.

All this has nothing to do with scholarship: it is about the mysterious and rather Jungian business of an evolving personal mythology.

For more scientific information, J. O. Urmson and Jonathan Rée, *The Concise Encyclopaedia of Western Philosophy and*

Philosophers (Routledge 1989) is one of the many useful guides available.

ARISTOTLE (384–322 BC), Greek philosopher. For him Plato's Forms exist only as they are realized or expressed in the objects of the world about us, and as the mental concepts of things that we have abstracted from our experience of those same objects. So far as the existence of a fully-Formed, stable and mind-independent external world is concerned, Aristotle is the classic 'realist', in the popular as well as the philosophical sense. Worldly, assured, confident, he launched metaphysics as the science of being.

   Some modern commentators point out how easily Aristotle can be reversed. Instead of the order of our concepts being derived from our experience of the world, maybe the order of the world is derived from *us*, as we impose our concepts upon it so as to make it known? Kant reversed Aristotle in this way.

page 65

AUGUSTINE, Bishop of Hippo (AD 354–430), North African Latin Bishop and the most influential Western Christian writer. In his *Confessions* and *Soliloquies* the main inventor of Western selfhood-before-God, with its lonely abyssal terrors and its need for authority. Standing behind Luther, Hamlet and Descartes, he may be seen as the first modernist; but more recently he has been called the first *post*-modernist, because his account of the plight of the individual self introduces a strain of vertigo, 'the bad infinite', and even nihilism, into Western consciousness.

page 112

BATAILLE, Georges (1897–1962), French – very French –writer, a valuable corrective to Anglo-Saxon utilitarianism and function-alism. An extremist, a theorist of excess, waste and the death-wish. A 'virulent nihilist'. *The Accursed Share, Theory of Religion, Eroticism*, etc.

pages 4, 76

BAUDRILLARD, Jean (1929–), French cultural theorist, and perhaps Bataille's il/legitimate successor: certainly equally original and perverse. In his thought a hyperbolical romantic conservative, a glittering black pessimist. A large, varied, developing output.

pages 107, 114

BENTHAM, Jeremy (1748–1832), English philosopher and re-former: psychological egoist, ethical utilitarian, inventor of the Panopticon, father of the scientific-humanist dream of the totally-planned, rational and optimized world. Comparable with such more recent figures as B. F. Skinner and H. J. Eysenck.

page 9

BERGSON, Henri, (1859–1941), French philosopher, of a generation which, like the American pragmatists, sought to rethink life, action, knowledge and time, after Darwin. Gilles Deleuze owes something to him.

pages 25, 97

BERKELEY, Bishop George (1685–1753), Irish philosopher. He sought to combat the rise of atheistic materialism, denying matter and arguing that our sense-experience is presented to us directly by God's creative thought. Thus he saw all the world as a 'divine visual language'. *Principles of Human Knowledge, Alciphron, Three Dialogues.*

pages 5, 22, 46, 59

DANTE (1265–1321), Italian poet. Still the best guide to the world-view of Western Christianity at its apogee.

pages 39, 64, 90

DARWIN, Charles (1809–1882), English biologist and 'the only great man who was a nice man'. *The Origin of Species*, the second volume of *The Descent of Man*, *The Expression of the Emotions*. Plagued by anxiety, lived in some seclusion, changed everything.

pages 20, 37, 96, 109

DAVIDSON, Donald (1917–), American philosopher. His rigorously naturalistic approach to language, knowledge and the mind has helped to turn Anglo-Saxon philosophy towards a new version of pragmatism. Best popularized by Rorty (*q.v.*).

pages 32ff.

DELEUZE, GILLES (1925–), French philosopher – of difference rather than sameness, of events rather than substances, and of Becoming rather than stable order. Obscure, intriguing, not yet well understood.

page 25

(1994)
DERRIDA, Jacques (1930–), French philosopher, especially of writing and interpretation – and therefore of the 'Arts', or literary studies.

pages 4, 57, 120

DESCARTES, Réne (1596–1650), French philosopher. Very successful, because he seemed to have overcome scepticism, to have made the world safe for the new mechanistic natural science, and to have preserved something very like Augustine's world-view. *Meditations on First Philosophy*.

pages 21, 45, 113

FOUCAULT, Michel (1926–1984), French historian of ideas and institutions. He took his analyses of the relationships between power and truth right down to the level of individual psychology. He has popularized the idea that our notions of gender and forms of selfhood are transient historical constructs, and that (as people say) 'the personal is also political'. Like Marx, whom he has superseded, he hints that for Westerners the Catholic Church has been the classic site for study of the relations between the production and control of truth and the maintenance and extension of power.

Foucault takes some of his ideas from Nietzsche, Bataille and Deleuze.

page 55

FREUD, Sigmund (1856–1939), Viennese psychologist, now to be read *not* as a pseudo-scientist, but as a brilliant reader and interpreter of people's language and body-language. Best book – still *The Interpretation of Dreams*.

pages 42, 73, 76, 90, 133

FEUERBACH, Ludwig A. (1804–1872), German philosopher. The most eloquent of the 'young Hegelians', who correctly grasped that Hegel's philosophy is best read as a dialectical humanism. His interpretation of Christianity as a humanist faith (in *The Essence of Christianity*) has not been refuted.

pages 2, 116

GALILEO, Galilei (1564–1642), Italian natural philosopher. His *Dialogues on the Two Chief Systems of the World* (1632) make up the earliest scientific book that is still a good read. He first gave to mathematical physics the special prestige it still enjoys.

page 74

HEGEL, G. W. F. (1770–1831), German Idealist philosopher, constructor of the ultimate totalizing system which, by being systematically ambiguous from bottom to top, postponed the death of God for fifty years. For verdicts upon him consult Schopenhauer, Kierkegaard or Nietzsche.

pages 62, 116, 128

HEIDEGGER, Martin (1889–1976), German philosopher. A touching, self-damaged figure, his late writings are now growing steadily in stature despite their deplorable obscurity. 'Language is the house of Being.'
In platonism, the philosopher has to be personally virtuous. But in these post-platonic days, not all philosophers are good people, alas.

pages 4, 12, 22, 68, 76, 113

HOBBES, Thomas (1588–1679), English philosopher. A materialist with a fine rude vigorous style, and a good example of a writer who takes an expressivist (and so non-realist) view of our language about God.

pages 74f.

JAMES, William (1842–1910), American pragmatist philosopher. Medically qualified, a fine psychologist and splendid prose writer, and the best example so far of a democratic philosopher. See his *Essays in Radical Empiricism*.

pages 2, 14, 22, 25, 69ff., 97

KANT, Immanuel (1724–1804), German philosopher. He asked how our mathematical physics is possible and answered, by reversing Aristotle (*q.v.*). *We* give all the orders; we impose Form upon the chaos of experience. Only thus is the world knowable by us. Kant was a contemporary of the French and American

Revolutions, and it was he (as Foucault might say) who gave birth to Man – Man the upright, autonomous legislator who makes himself, society and the world transparent to his own Reason.

Kant is not wholly a villain, however. In the Dialectic of *The Critique of Pure Reason*, his 'transcendental theology' is a fine statement of non-realistic theism; and in his later book on religion he begins the move from ecclesiastical theology to kingdom-theology.

pages 5, 19, 20, 24, 34, 59, 63, 106, 112, 128

KIERKEGAARD, Søren (1813–1855), Danish philosopher. Highly literary and an early postmodernist, he sought to undermine Hegel's totalizing rationalism by showing that for each individual the question of the meaning of his own existence 'before God' comes first of all, and radically *precedes* rational, speculative thought. Read the *Concluding Unscientific Post-script*, Part Two, chs 1–3.

pages 22, 62, 112

LACAN, Jacques (1901–1981). French psychoanalyst, difficult in more ways than one, who transformed Freud's legacy. The Unconscious is cultural: it is 'structured like a language', and the self is constituted within language. See *Écrits*, *The Four Fundamental Concepts of Psychoanalysis* and *The Language of Self: The Function of Language in Psychoanalysis*.

pages 38, 44

LOCKE, John (1632–1704), English philosopher and apologist for Whiggery and free trade. Something of a bogey, for his scientific realism, for his empiricist assumption of the innocence of raw experience as it enters the pure vacancy of an unbiased English mind, and for his adoption of too much from Descartes.

page 25

MILL, John Stuart (1806–1873), English radical philosopher of Bentham's party, but partly humanized by suffering, by the Romantic movement and by Harriet Taylor. Best for his opposition to intuitionism and his insistence upon argument in all ethical and social questions. *Utilitarianism* ch. v. contains what almost amounts to a Nietzschean genealogy of Justice.

page 9

NEWTON, Isaac (1642–1727), English mathematical physicist, of Trinity College, Cambridge. A sad figure: to have triumphed so greatly in physics, and to have failed so dismally in philosophy, in religious thought, and in respect of his own personal happiness.

pages 20, 45, 54

NIETZSCHE, Friedrich (1844–1900), German philosopher. Such gifts, such a catastrophe. By sheer determination Nietzsche made himself into perhaps the greatest human being and writer of modern times; but the effort destroyed him, and the work is as open to a thoroughly evil interpretation as to any other. So was it rational of him to aim for the top? Best books: *Daybreak* and *The Gay Science*.

pages 2, 4, 10, 22, 25, 58, 61, 89, 97, 112, 116, 128

PARMENIDES of Elea (*c.* 515–460 BC), Greek philosopher. The first great philosopher of Being.

page 74

PASCAL, Blaise (1623–1663), French mathematician. Another brilliant, eloquent, damaged character: a 'fideist', someone who claims that in matters of religious truth pure non-rational 'faith' is the right and proper way of knowing.

pages 37, 58

PLATO (427–347 BC), Greek philosopher, whose literary corpus was the dominant achievement in the history of philosophy until the time of Kant and Hegel. His realistic account of the Forms, as together composing an eternal Order of Objective Reason, was used by him and others to justify the detestable belief in an objective truth of things and objective values, which in turn has justified the elitism, the authoritarianism and the power-worship that have disfigured so much of our history and have rotted away our religion.

Those who wish to escape from Plato's influence must either prove his leading doctrines wrong, or find ways of reading him against himself. Because he wrote in Dialogue form and is highly literary, the latter strategy is probably smarter. Best dialogue, *The Republic*.

pages 2, 10, 22, 54, 73, 98, 106

RORTY, Richard (1931–), American philosophical writer. Anti-foundationalist, 'post-philosopher', admirable stylist. *Philosophy and the Mirror of Nature, Consequences of Pragmatism, Philosophical Papers*.

page 30

RUSSELL, Bertrand (1872–1970), the last major British Empiricist philosopher, now somewhat in eclipse.

pages 5, 23

SARTRE (1905–1980), French philosopher. The first genuinely self-styled 'existentialist' – a term that died with him. 'Man' is a 'useless project', 'condemned to be free': Sartre was an extreme Cartesian and romantic individualist, the last of the 'I-philosophers' who started from the individual self. The next generation argued that the self is not primary, but is produced within the movement of language and history.

pages 58, 76, 112

SCHOPENHAUER, Arthur (1788–1860), German philosopher. A conscious atheist, a follower of Kant, and an admirer of Indian thought, he was also an Anglophile. A sarcastic old curmudgeon and a heterosexual misogynist, he was of a type familiar, and even much-loved, in England.

Nietzsche says that every metaphysical system is a spiritual autobiography. Indeed: for Schopenhauer's Universe has the surface appearance of things well-ordered, but down in the depths the Will is perennially in turmoil, at odds with itself. He was like that, poor old devil.

pages 25, 63

SPINOZA, Baruch (or Benedict de) (1632–1677), Dutch philosopher. He accepted the new hegemony of mathematical physics, and produced a rigorously-argued metaphysical system which is also a classic text of religious-naturalism.

Spinoza's mysticism is a mysticism of unity and rational necessity – a bit lifeless, Nietzsche thought.

pages 5, 26, 63

WITTGENSTEIN, Ludwig (1889–1951), Austrian philosopher. A pupil of Russell, he began as an extreme realist, trying to spell out exactly how a bit of language could specify, and copy the shape of, a bit of non-language. Later he repudiated realism: but to this day most people find non-realism hard to understand. See the *Philosophical Investigations*.

pages 15, 22, 30f., 35ff., 69, 76, 93, 133

Note

At the proof stage I add the names of David Hume (pages 5, 22, 69) and Heraclitus (p.4). Both are surely part of my canon, and should have been included.

Glossary

In the main text of this book, technical terms are very few. But a number of innocuous-sounding words are used in special ways which may lead to misunderstanding. Hence this brief glossary.

Becoming   The world to which we have access through our sense-experience – the 'phenomenal' world, the world of appearance, the contingent world, the word of everything that comes to be and passes away – has been called since Plato the world of Becoming. He regarded it as unreal and unsatisfactory, and sought to turn our attention away from it towards the intellectual world, the 'noumenal', really Real and timeless world of the Forms.

Sealed into Christian thought, this contrast between the world of time and change and a better world beyond it continued to be very influential until the nineteenth century. But then Nietzsche's proclamation of 'the innocence of Becoming' marked the beginning of an attempt to get rid of the old fear of time that for so long had led people to associate change with decay, transience with corruption, and flesh with frailty. Gradually, in the later Heidegger and others, Being itself becomes a verb, Be-ing, and the Fountain, the ceaseless forthcoming of Becoming, becomes the object of beatific contemplation. The transient and the eternal coincide.

Constructivism   In the philosophy of mathematics, the position that requires all mathematical entities and truths to be 'constructed' or proved. Nothing is accepted merely on the basis of its supposed self-evidence to intuition.

Recently, a similar position has appeared in general epistemology (= theory of knowledge). Constructivists decline to accept the claim that some category or principle is self-evident, or natural, or basic: they demand a supporting argument in all cases.

Constructivists thus stand in the Kantian tradition: consistently critical thinking leads in the end to the conclusion that we have ourselves built *all* of our knowledge and our vision of the world. By trial and error we have slowly developed ways of thinking, ways of world-building, that are good for us because they help us to live together, to survive and even to flourish. So constructivism is very close to pragmatism.

Foundationalism A recent and pejorative label for a myth and a style of thinking associated with Descartes, Kant and others. Every knowledge-system is regarded as being like a building; it needs strong foundations. These should consist of a set of necessary truths, laid down and approved by philosophers, that define the ground-plan of the subject.

This makes philosophy itself foundational for culture, but Richard Rorty and others have been arguing that our culture is no longer – if it ever was – aware of needing philosophers to do such a job for it.

God Outside protected religious slots, the word *God* is now not much used in everyday language. Empirical study finds three main uses: (1) an expletive-expressive use in such phrases as *Good God!*, *God knows!*, *For God's sake!*; (2) as a shorthand way of referring to the religious concern: God symbolizes religion in general, and the claims of religion; and (3), as a symbol of moral authority and as the ground of moral obligation.

Building on these remaining everyday uses of the word, *the non-realist doctrine of God* views God as the religious ideal, a symbol that incorporates our values and represents to us the goal of the religious life. It is the only coherent view of God currently available to us.

According to the argument of the present book, there is no subjective immortality or subjective redemption. The reason for this is that our transience, and a certain disharmony of aims between the various sub-systems of which we are composed, is constitutive of our very life. So we have to go out of ourselves and seek redemption through self-expression.

Accordingly it is symbolically appropriate to picture God as an objective person, love for whom draws us out of ourselves and into expression. But God is not part of general philosophy. He is only a religiously useful and valuable myth, and it is sufficient in the philosophy of religion to explain how he functions as the 'imaginary focus' (*focus imaginarius*, a phrase from Kant) of the religious life.

Humanism   A particularly complicated word with a long history. Because ordinary language is still surprisingly religious and moralistic in its concerns, there is a certain tendency to see humanism as the Other of religion or theism, and therefore as 'worshipping Man', 'putting Man in the place of God', and so on.

In the present book we use *humanism* in the sense popularized by William James and his younger friend and ally F. C. S. Schiller (1864–1937). By using the word we remind ourselves that the human world, which is the world of human life and language, human feelings and purposes, is outsideless, and everything is constructed within it. Our conceptual frameworks, our modes of reasoning, our beliefs and values, our knowledge-systems, our art and our religion are all of our own construction, and are to be evaluated by the criterion of their utility in serving the purposes of our life.

Life   A challenge to the lexicographer. Distinguish four main groups of uses: (1) the various properties and capacities that distinguish living organisms from inanimate things; (2) the temporal process of living; (3) the whole world of life, considered as a milieu or an Other with which we are in a constant process of exchange: *How's life?*, we say: *That's life!*; and (4), the whole course of a life from birth to death, the subject-matter of a biography.

In the present book we join those philosophers who are saying that if in the future we are able to revive metaphysics, it will have to take the form of philosophy of life.

Materialism   In everyday language this word is used either to characterize the outlook of a person who is keen on the goods that money can buy, or to describe a world-view that sees everything as being made of thick, heavy, material stuff. But in current philosophy *materialism* means much the same as *naturalism*.

Metaphysics   In Aristotle, the science of being as such. Also the study of first principles, of substance, of the Real as a whole. In the twentieth century the most interesting and influential writing about the history of Western metaphysics has been that of Heidegger and Derrida.

Naturalism   Usually the doctrine that everything can in principle be explained in natural terms, without having recourse to anything supernatural. Hence, the doctrine that rejects any notion of degrees of being or reality, and instead seeks to bring everything down to one level. Such a one-level view of things is often called *monism* or (nowadays) *materialism*.

Richard Rorty has described naturalism as the doctrine that 'everything is contingent' or 'everything is the product of time and chance.' I have preferred to say rather that the human life-world is outsideless, finite but unbounded like the dictionary and like the Universe of physics. Everything then is immanent, and naturalism is simply thoroughgoing immanentism. Everything is inside because there *is* no Outside.

Pragmatism   A maxim or style in philosophy originated by the Americans C. S. Peirce (1839–1914) and William James (1842–1910). It is naturalistic and functionalist. We should check out the meanings of all words and theories in terms of their 'sensible effects' or their 'cash-value' in life. True beliefs are those beliefs that we do well to be guided by.

In seeing all our utterances and ideas as tools we use for doing jobs with, pragmatism in some ways foreshadowed the later thought of Wittgenstein, who indeed liked James' work. And in recent years much of Anglo-Saxon analytical philosophy has been turning toward neo-pragmatism.

Realism Philosophers have used the term realism in many different ways. Plato evidently believed that his world of Forms (or 'Universals') really existed, independently of any mind, whereas *conceptualists* say they are just thoughts, and *nominalists* that they are just words. In mathematics, realists say that truth is discovered, non-realists that it is invented. With regard to 'the external world', realists say that physical objects exist quite independently of our experience of them, whereas *phenomenalists, subjective idealists* and the like deny this.

British thought has been particularly troubled about the question of realism, because so many of the leading British thinkers have been *empiricists*, who have held that all our knowledge of 'synthetic' or substantial truths is ultimately derived from experience, and must in principle be testable against experience. But how can we claim to have been given *within* experience sufficient evidence for the belief that something or other exists quite *apart from* our experience? So the question of realism has troubled not only Berkeley and Hume, but more recently Mill, Russell and Ayer. In different ways, all five were non-realists, or not-quite-realists.

With the turn to language in post-war thought the issues have been redefined in 'humanist' and linguistic terms. Here realists will say that the theoretical entities of science, religion, morality, etc. do exist (or at least purport to exist) independently of the language in which we speak of them. For the realist there are truths *out there*, beyond the range of the truth that human beings have so far determined. But for the anti-realist we are the only makers of meanings, truths and values, and our theoretical postulates, such as God, gravity and justice, have no being apart from the language in which we speak of them and the practical uses to which we put it.

The reader will have noted that realism is false and anti-realism is true, *but it is paradoxical to say so!* Since anti-realists deny real truth out there, their doctrine cannot really be True. The crux of the present book's argument seeks to escape that paradox by requiring the text to be read aloud. The vocalization becomes part of a truth that is shown, not stated.

Anti-realism The contradictory of realism, its straight antithesis: my doctrine, but paradoxical, as we have seen.

148

Non-realism The contrary of realism, any doctrine other than realism. Because non-realism does not give rise to such sudden and disconcerting paradoxes as anti-realism, it is more suitable for popularization.

Subjectivity The state or condition of being a subject of experience. In early-nineteenth-century German idealist philosophy there was an interest in unifying two visions of the world, the old one focussed around God as the infinite divine subject, and the newer one focussed around the finite human subject. There was at that time a real danger of the self's becoming crazily over-inflated, even deified. So in the present book I have sought to avoid that danger by 'the double reduction' that resolves the self down into the flux of the world as much as it takes all the world up into the self.